W9-ADS-963

why translation matters

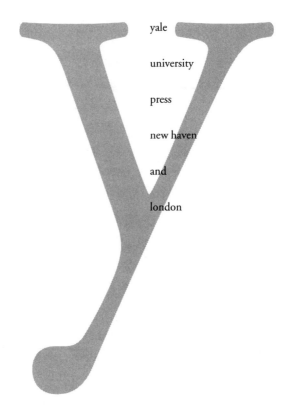

yale

university

press

new haven

and

london

edith

grossman

why

translation

matters

Published with assistance from the Louis Stern Memorial
Fund.

"Why X Matters" and the yX logo are trademarks of Yale
University.

Set in Adobe Garamond type by Keystone Typesetting, Inc.,
Orwigsburg, Pennsylvania. Printed in the United States of
America.

Library of Congress Cataloging-in-Publication Data
Grossman, Edith.
Why translation matters / Edith Grossman.
    p.   cm. — (Why X matters)
Includes bibliographical references and index.
ISBN 978-0-300-12656-3 (cloth : alk. paper) 1. Literature—
Translations. 2. Translating and interpreting. I. Title.
PN241.G75 2010
418′.02—dc22   2009026510

A catalogue record for this book is available from the British
Library.

This paper meets the requirements of ANSI/NISO
Z39.48-1992 (Permanence of Paper).

10   9   8   7   6   5   4   3   2   1

selected translations by edith grossman

Alvaro Mutis, *The Adventures and Misadventures of Maqroll*

Carlos Fuentes, *Happy Families*

Antonio Muñoz Molina, *A Manuscript of Ashes*

Santiago Roncagliolo, *Red April*

Eliseo Alberto, *Caracol Beach*

Augusto Monterroso, *Complete Works and Other Stories*

contents

preface

In 2007 Professor María Rosa Menocal invited me to Yale University to initiate an annual lecture series under the auspices of the Whitney Center for the Humanities. The general title of the series was to be Why X Matters, the X depending on the field or area of specialization of the person delivering the lectures. In my case, naturally, that fearsome unknown quantity was translation.

I agreed immediately. I have always enjoyed my visits to Yale and the opportunity to talk to the intelligent, enthusiastic students and committed faculty I meet there. Then too, I invariably take great pleasure in speaking about translation, in all kinds of settings, formal and informal, casual and academic.

The introduction and first two chapters of the book are based on three talks I gave at the Whitney Center in the spring of 2008. The final chapter, "Translating Poetry," was written especially for this volume. It was inspired by recent work I had either completed or was about to begin: the selection of Renaissance poems I had translated a few years earlier for Norton, which were published in 2006 in *The Golden Age: Poems of the Spanish Renaissance,* and, under the aegis of the Guggenheim Foundation, the major translating project—Luis de Góngora's *Soledades*—that would occupy most of my time in 2009. I had frequently discussed the issues involved in the translation of fiction, but preparing this book seemed the perfect moment to begin to address the even more problematic question of how one transfers a poem from one language to another.

I hope the reading of these essays inspires other ways to think about and talk about translation. My intention is to stimulate a new consideration of an area of literature that is too often ignored, misunderstood, or misrepresented. As the world seems to grow smaller and more interdependent and interconnected while, at the same time, nations and peoples paradoxically become increasingly antagonistic to one another, translation has an important function to fulfill that I believe must be cherished and nurtured. Translation not only plays its important traditional role as the means that allows us access to literature originally written in one of the countless languages we cannot read, but it also represents a concrete literary presence with the crucial capacity to ease and make more meaningful our relationships to those with whom we may not have had a connection before. Translation always helps us to know, to see from a different angle, to attribute new value to what once may have been unfamiliar. As nations and as individuals, we have a critical need for that kind of understanding and insight. The alternative is unthinkable.

introduction:

why

translation

matters

No problem is as consubstantial
with literature and its modest
mystery as the one posed by
translation.

—JORGE LUIS BORGES,
"Las versiones homéricas"

To introduce these essays, I thought it would be useful to pass along some incidental information about my background and the circumstances that led me, however indirectly, to a career in translation.

When I was young—a high school student—it was not my intention to be a translator. I knew I wanted to learn languages and had a vague idea about being an interpreter. (I wasn't quite sure what the difference between the two professions was, but interpreting sounded more exciting; it suggested travel, exotic places, important events, world-shaking conferences at the United Nations.) As an undergraduate at the University of Pennsylvania, I changed direction and decided my ambition was to be a literary critic and scholar, even though, operating under the mistaken assumption that apparently simple poetry was simple to translate, I do recall submitting a few poems by Juan Ramón Jiménez and, if I remember correctly, Gustavo Adolfo Bécquer, to the campus literary magazine. I embarked on an academic career, served my time in several graduate schools, and moved from a focus on medieval and baroque peninsular verse, first the Galician-Portuguese love lyrics and then the sonnets of Francisco de Quevedo, to contemporary Latin American poetry, a change brought about by my first reading of works by Pablo Neruda, and soon after that César Vallejo. (I came on this stunning poetry fairly late in my student career: I have no memory of reading any Latin American literature written after the Mexican Revolution until I made the cross-country trek to Berkeley.) Neruda's *Residencia en la tierra* in particular was a revelation that altered radically the professional direction I followed and actually changed the tenor of my life. It elucidated for me, as if for the first time, the possibilities of poetry in a contemporary environment. Above all, it underscored the central position of Latin America in the literature of the world, its impact made possible and even more telling by means of translation.

I began teaching while I was a graduate student, and then continued giving classes full-time when I moved back east and enrolled in New York University. During most of this time I was thinking more about my dissertation than about translation. But one day Ronald Christ, a friend who edited the magazine *Review,* the publication of the organization once called the Center for Inter-American Relations and now known as the Americas Society, asked me to translate a story by the Argentine Macedonio Fernández, a writer of the generation just before Borges. I said I was a critic, not a translator, and he said that might be true, but he thought I could do a good job with the piece. I agreed to translate it, more out of curiosity about its wildly eccentric author and the process of translation than for any other reason. I discovered to my surprise that I not only enjoyed the work more than I had imagined but could do it at home, an arrangement that seemed very attractive then, and still does.

My translation of Macedonio's "The Surgery of Psychic Removal" was published in *Review* in 1973. From that time on, I moonlighted as a translator of poetry and fiction in a fairly regular way while I sunlighted as a college instructor until 1990, when I left teaching to devote myself full-time to translation. I have been a visiting professor several times since then, and when I am not teaching I miss being in a classroom and talking to students, but my main concentration and professional focus have been on translation. And I have been very fortunate: I have liked, and often loved, practically every piece of writing I have brought over into English, and after all these years I still find the work intriguing, mysterious, and endlessly challenging.

Why translation matters: the subject is so huge, so complex, and so dear to my heart that I have decided to begin my approach to it by answering the implicit question with another question, using the technique of query-as-response—a traditional, perhaps time-honored method of indicating the almost impenetrable difficulty of a subject, and certainly, as every pedagogue knows, a good way to delay and even confound the questioner until you can think of an acceptable answer that has at least a glimmer of coherence. My variation on that traditional ploy consists of breaking the question into still smaller components in order to refocus the inquiry and ask not only why translation matters, but also whether it matters at all, and if in fact it does have importance, who exactly cares about it. The answers that emerge may really depend on how the questions are formulated: Why, for example, does translation matter to translators, authors, and readers? Why does it not matter to most publishers and book reviewers? What is its relevance to the literary tradition in any number of languages? What is its contribution to the civilized life of the world? My attempt to devise a response to these various elements constitutes a kind of preliminary appraisal of some of the thorny, ongoing, apparently never-to-be-resolved problems that surround the question of literary translation, beginning with the old chestnut of whether it is possible at all, and moving on to what it actually does, and what its proper place in the universe of literature should be.

I believe that serious professional translators, often in private, think of themselves—forgive me, I mean ourselves—as writers, no matter what else may cross our minds when we ponder the work we do, and I also believe we are correct to do so. Is this sheer presumption, a heady kind of immodesty on our part? What exactly do we literary translators do to justify the notion that the term "writer" actually applies to us? Aren't we simply the humble, anonymous handmaids-and-men of literature, the grateful, ever-obsequious servants of the publishing industry? In the most resounding yet decorous terms I can muster, the answer is no, for the most fundamental description of what translators do is that we write—or perhaps rewrite—in language B a work of literature originally composed in language A, hoping that readers of the second language—I mean, of course, readers of the translation—will perceive the text, emotionally and artistically, in a manner that parallels and corresponds to the esthetic experience of its first readers. This is the translator's grand ambition. Good translations approach that purpose. Bad translations never leave the starting line.

As a first step toward accomplishing so exemplary an end, translators need to develop a keen sense of style in both languages, honing and expanding our critical awareness of the emotional impact of words, the social aura that surrounds them, the setting and mood that informs them, the atmosphere they create. We struggle to sharpen and elaborate our perception of the connotations and implications behind basic denotative meaning in a process not dissimilar to the efforts writers make to increase their familiarity with and competence in a given literary idiom.

Writing, like any other artistic practice, is a vocation that calls to deep, resonating parts of our psyches; it is not something translators or writers can be dissuaded from doing or would abandon easily. It seems strikingly paradoxical, but although translators obviously are writing someone else's work, there is no shame or subterfuge in this despite the peculiar disparagement and continual undervaluing of what we do by some publishers and many reviewers.

As William Carlos Williams said in a letter written in 1940 to the art critic and poet Nicolas Calas (and my thanks to Jonathan Cohen, the scholar of inter-American literature, for sharing the quotation with me):

> If I do original work all well and good. But if I can say it (the matter of form I mean) by translating the work of others that also is valuable. What difference does it make?

The undeniable reality is that the work becomes the translator's (while simultaneously and mysteriously somehow remaining the work of the original author) as we transmute it into a second language. Perhaps *transmute* is the wrong verb; what we do is not an act of magic, like altering base metals into precious ones, but the result of a series of creative decisions and imaginative acts of criticism. In the process of translating, we endeavor to hear the first version of the work as profoundly and completely as possible, struggling to discover the linguistic charge, the structural rhythms, the subtle implications, the complexities of meaning and suggestion in vocabulary and phrasing, and the ambient, cultural inferences and conclusions these tonalities allow us to extrapolate. This is a kind of reading as deep as any encounter with a literary text can be.

For example, consider fiction. Dialogue contains often nuanced though sometimes egregious indications of the class, status, and education of the characters, not to mention their intelligence and emotional state; significant intentions and sonorities abound in the narration and in the descriptive portions of the work; there may be elements of irony or satire; the rhythm of the prose (long, flowing periods or short, crisp phrases) and the tone of the writing (colloquialisms, elevated diction, pomposities, slang, elegance, substandard usage) are pivotal stylistic devices, and it is incumbent upon the translator to apprehend the ways in which these instrumentalities further the purposes of the fiction, the revelation of character, the progress of the action.

To varying degrees, all attentive readers do this, consciously or unconsciously. Certainly students and teachers of literature attempt to achieve this kind of profound analysis in every paper they write, every lecture they give. How, then, does the endeavor of the translator differ from that of any careful reader, not to mention harried students and their equally hard-pressed instructors? The unique factor in the experience of translators is that we not only are listeners to the text, hearing the author's voice in the mind's ear, but speakers of a second text—the translated work—who repeat what we have heard, though in another language, a language with its own literary tradition, its own cultural accretions, its own lexicon and syntax, its own historical experience, all of which must be treated with as much respect, esteem, and appreciation as we bring to the language of the original writer. Our purpose is to re-create as far as possible, within the alien system of a second language, all the characteristics, vagaries, quirks, and stylistic peculiarities of the work we are translating. And we do this by analogy—that is, by finding comparable, not identical, characteristics, vagaries, quirks, and stylistic peculiarities in the second language. Repeating the work in any other way—for example, by succumbing to the literalist fallacy and attempting to duplicate the text in another language, following a pattern of word-for-word transcription— would lead not to a translation but to a grotesque variation on Borges's Pierre Menard, who rewrites his own *Don Quixote* that coincides word for word with Cervantes' original, though it is considered superior to the original because of its modernity. Furthermore, a mindless, literalist translation would constitute a serious breach of contract. There isn't a self-respecting publisher in the world who would not reject a manuscript framed in this way. It is not acceptable, readable, or faithful, as the letters of agreement demand, though it certainly may have its own perverse originality.

To cite Walter Benjamin in his essay "The Task of the Translator,"

> No translation would be possible if in its ultimate essence it strove for likeness to the original. . . . For just as the tenor and significance of the great works of literature undergo a complete transformation over the centuries, the mother tongue of the translator is transformed as well. While a poet's words endure in his own language, even the greatest translation is destined to become part of the growth of its own language and eventually to be absorbed by its renewal. Translation is so far removed from being the sterile equation of two dead languages that of all literary forms it is the one charged with the special mission of watching over the maturing process of the original language and the birth pangs of its own. (74–75)

And as Ralph Manheim, the great translator from German, so famously said, translators are like actors who speak the lines as the author would if the author could speak English. As one would expect from so gifted a practitioner of the art, Manheim's observation on translation is wonderfully insightful and revelatory. Whatever else it may be, translation in Manheim's formulation is a kind of interpretive performance, bearing the same relationship to the original text as the actor's work does to the script, the performing musician's to the composition. This image of performance may account for the fact that, surprisingly enough, I always seem to conceive of and discuss the translating process as essentially auditory, something immediately available to other people, as opposed to a silent, solitary process. I think of the author's voice and the sound of the text, then of my obligation to hear both as clearly and profoundly as possible, and finally of my equally pressing need to speak the piece in a second language. Especially in the translation of poetry, which I discuss at greater length in chapter 3, this practice is not purely metaphorical. It is, instead, an integral part of my actual approach to the interpretation of a poem in Spanish and its rendering into English. In my case, the work tends to be done viva voce.

We read translations all the time, but of all the interpretive arts, it is fascinating and puzzling to realize that only translation has to fend off the insidious, damaging question of whether or not it is, can be, or should be possible. It would never occur to anyone to ask whether it is feasible for an actor to perform a dramatic role or a musician to interpret a piece of music. Of course it is feasible, just as it is possible for a translator to rewrite a work of literature in another language. Can it be done well? I think so, as do my translating colleagues, but there are other, more antipathetic opinions. Yet even the most virulent, mean-spirited critic reluctantly admits on occasion that some few decent translations do appear from time to time. And the very concept of world literature as a discipline fit for academic study depends on the availability of translations. Translation occupies a central and prominent position in the conceptualization of a universal, enlightened civilization, and, no small accomplishment, it almost defines the European Renaissance. The "rebirth" we all have studied at one time or another began as the translation into Latin and then the vernacular languages of the ancient Greek philosophy and science that had been lost to Christian Europe for centuries. Poets of the late fifteenth, sixteenth, and seventeenth centuries—for example, the Spaniards Garcilaso de la Vega and Fray Luis de León—routinely translated and adapted classical and then Italian works, and these versions of Horace or Virgil or Petrarch were included as a matter of course in collections of their original poems.

Translation is crucial to our sense of ourselves as serious readers, and as literate, educated men and women we would find the absence of translations to read and study inconceivable. There are roughly six thousand extant languages in the world. Let us hypothesize that approximately one thousand of them are written. Not even the most gifted linguist could read complex literary texts in one thousand languages. We tend to be in awe of the few people who can read even ten languages well, and it clearly is an astonishing feat, although we have to remember that if there were no translations, even those multilingual prodigies would be deprived of any encounter with works written in the 990 tongues they don't know. If this is true for the linguistically gifted, imagine the impact that the disappearance of translations would have on the rest of us. Translation expands our ability to explore through literature the thoughts and feelings of people from another society or another time. It permits us to savor the transformation of the foreign into the familiar and for a brief time to live outside our own skins, our own preconceptions and misconceptions. It expands and deepens our world, our consciousness, in countless, indescribable ways.

The translation of their works is also of critical importance to writers around the world, promising them a significant increase in readership. One of the many reasons writers write—though certainly not the only one—is to communicate with and affect as many people as possible. Translation expands that number exponentially, allowing more and more readers to be touched by an author's work. For writers whose first language is limited in terms of how many people speak it, translation is indispensable for achieving an audience of consequential size. For those whose first language is spoken by millions, though a decisive number of them may be illiterate or so impoverished that buying books is not an option, translation is also an imperative. It is one of the preposterous ironies of our current literary situation that despite the pitifully low number of translations published each year in the United States, the United Kingdom, and the rest of the English-speaking world compared, say, with the industrialized nations of western Europe or Latin America, the English-language market is the one most writers and their agents crave for their books. English is the world's lingua franca in commerce, technology, and diplomacy, and it tends to be spoken in places where literacy is prevalent and people are prosperous enough to purchase books, even though the number of book buyers seems to decrease steadily. Some years ago Philip Roth estimated that there are four thousand people in the United States who buy books, and he went on to say that once you have sold your work to them and the libraries, your run is essentially ended. On optimistic days, I assume Roth was being characteristically sardonic. At other times, I am not so sure.

One of the double-edged canards about the Nobel Prize is that no writer who has not been translated into English can hope even to be considered for the prize in literature, because English is the one language all the judges can read. This notion actually seems to be true for the use of the book in other media, such as film. A book that has not been translated into English has little likelihood of ever being made into a widely distributed movie.

Translation affects creative artists in another, perhaps less obvious but much more important and extraordinarily conse-quential way—one that goes far beyond questions of financial reward, no matter how significant that may be. As Walter Ben-jamin indicates in the passage cited earlier, literary translation infuses a language with influences, alterations, and combina-tions that would not have been possible without the presence of translated foreign literary styles and perceptions, the material significance and heft of literature that lies outside the territory of the purely monolingual. In other words, the influence of translated literature has a revivifying and expansive effect on what is hideously called the "target language," the language into which the text is translated.

In 1964 Robert Bly wrote an essay entitled "The Surprise of Neruda," in which he speaks directly to this issue:

> We tend to associate the modern imagination with the jerky imag-ination, which starts forward, stops, turns around, switches from subject to subject. In Neruda's poems, the imagination drives for-ward, joining the entire poem in a rising flow of imaginative en-ergy. . . . He is a new kind of creature moving about under the surface of everything.
>
> Moving under the earth, he knows everything from the bottom up (which is the right way to learn the nature of a thing) and therefore is never at a loss for its name. Compared to him, the American poet resembles a blind man moving about above the ground from tree to tree, from house to house, feeling each thing for a long time, and then calling out "house," when we already know it's a house. (quoted in Cohen, 28)

The impact of the kind of artistic discovery that translation enables is profoundly important to the health and vitality of any language and any literature. It may be one of the reasons that histories of national literatures so often seem to exclude supremely significant connections among writers. "National literature" is a narrowing, confining concept based on the distinction between native and foreign, which is certainly a valid and useful differentiation in some areas and under certain circumstances, but in writing it is obviated by translation, which dedicates itself to denying and negating the impact of divine punishment for the construction of the Tower of Babel, or at least to overcoming its worst divisive effects. Translation asserts the possibility of a coherent, unified experience of literature in the world's multiplicity of languages. At the same time, translation celebrates the differences among languages and the many varieties of human experience and perception they can express. I do not believe this is a contradiction. Rather, it testifies to the comprehensive, inclusive embrace of both literature and translation.

One example among many of the fruitful exchange among languages brought about by translation is the ongoing connection between William Faulkner and Gabriel García Márquez. When he was a young man, García Márquez had an insatiable appetite for Faulkner's fiction and devoured his novels in Spanish translations, along with the books of many other authors writing in other languages. Over the years he has spoken often of Faulkner as his favorite English-language author—the subject of a long conversation between the Colombian and former president Bill Clinton (who had claimed that *One Hundred Years of Solitude* was the greatest novel of the past fifty years and called it his favorite work of fiction) at a dinner in William Styron's house on Martha's Vineyard in the summer of 1995. Carlos Fuentes was also present, and when he said that his favorite book was *Absalom, Absalom,* Clinton stood and recited from memory part of Benjy's monologue from *The Sound and the Fury.*

In *Living to Tell the Tale,* García Márquez's reading of *Light in August* runs like a leitmotif through his narrative of the trip he makes with his mother to sell the family house in Aracataca: "I already had read, in translation, and in borrowed editions, all the books I would have needed to learn the novelist's craft. . . . William Faulkner was the most faithful of my tutelary demons" (4, 6). Then he goes on to say: "I stayed in my room to read . . . books I obtained by chance and luck. . . . These [were] like bread warm from the oven, printed in Buenos Aires in new translations after the long hiatus in publishing because of the Second World War. In this way I discovered, to my good fortune, the already very-much-discovered Jorge Luis Borges, D. H. Lawrence and Aldous Huxley, Graham Greene and Gilbert Chesterton, William Irish and Katherine Mansfield, and many others" (245–246). Of James Joyce's *Ulysses* he writes: "It not only was the discovery of a genuine world that I never suspected inside me, but it also provided invaluable technical help to me in freeing language and in handling time and structures in my books" (247). And finally, this is how he describes the effect of reading Kafka for the first time: "I never again slept with my former serenity. The book was Franz Kafka's *The Metamorphosis,* in the false translation by Borges published by Losada in Buenos Aires, that determined a new direction for my life from its first line, which today is one of the great devices in world literature" (249). He may have called the translation "false" because, as he describes what he learned from Borges, all an author had to do was to write something for it to be true. In any event, in these brief passages, this remarkable novelist memorably evokes the breadth and vividness of a young writer's education in the craft of writing fiction, an initiation that would not have been possible without the existence of literary translations. These books, and all the other books he read, had a defining impact on his formation as a writer and allowed him to read as an apprentice to authors who in fact served as long-distance mentors.

Someone once called Faulkner the best-known Latin American writer in English, a description that may be more than a mere witticism. He seems to have inherited and then transferred into

English the expansive Cervantean style that has had so profound an influence, both positive and negative, on all subsequent Spanish-language writers. Moreover, Cervantes created the form and shape of modern fiction, a genre transformation of fundamental importance regardless of the fiction writer's language. The development of the novel in Europe, especially in eighteenth-century England and in the seminal work of Henry Fielding, grew directly out of the model of *Don Quixote,* which was translated almost immediately after publication. Thomas Shelton's English version, published in 1611, was the first translation into any language of the first part of Cervantes' novel, which appeared in 1605. The speculation that Shakespeare intended to write a play based on the adventures of Cardenio, the protagonist of one of the interpolated narratives in the first part of *Don Quixote,* or actually did write the play, though it unfortunately has been lost, becomes especially intriguing for our purposes because of the presence and success of Shelton's translation in England, which initiated the long, multifaceted history of Cervantes' influence on the growth of the novel, on the way novelists write, and certainly on the way Faulkner wrote.

There is no question that in the mid-twentieth century, Faulkner was the most important contemporary English-language writer in Latin America. His sonorous, eloquent, baroque style with its Cervantean resonances felt familiar to

Spanish-speaking readers, but I believe that even more decisive for his profound importance to the development of the Latin American novel, above all to the literary phenomenon called the Boom, was Faulkner's mythic, megahistorical, multigenerational vision of the land and the people who live on it. Not only García Márquez but Carlos Fuentes, Mario Vargas Llosa, and a host of other contemporary Latin American novelists owe a serious debt to Faulkner (and certainly to Cervantes). None of this rich literary cross-fertilization could have happened if Cervantes, Faulkner, and so many others had never been translated.

By the same token, it is impossible to conceive of the contemporary novel in English without taking García Márquez into account (not to mention Jorge Luis Borges and Julio Cortázar). The influence of García Márquez's writing—presumably in translation, as Faulkner's influence in Latin America undoubtedly took place for the most part in Spanish—is evident in a gamut of prominent writers like Toni Morrison, Salman Rushdie, Don de Lillo, and Michael Chabon, to name only a few. It is wonderful to contemplate, isn't it: the freedom García Márquez discovered in Joyce, and the structural and technical lessons he learned from him and from Faulkner, have been passed on to a younger generation of English-language fiction writers through the translated impact of the Colombian's writing. The innovative process of discovery that has allowed major writers to flex authorial muscles beyond the limitations of a single language and a single literary tradition would not have been possible without access to translated books. Translation is, in fact, a powerful, pervasive force that broadens and deepens a writer's perception of style, technique, and structure by allowing him or her to enter literary worlds not necessarily found in one national or linguistic tradition. Far beyond essentially pernicious anxieties of influence, writers learn their craft from one another, just as painters and musicians do. The days of direct apprenticeship are over, for the most part, except, of course, in formal, academic settings (creative writing programs, studio courses, or conservatory study, for example), but artists can find mentors in other ways. The more books from more places that are available to fledgling authors, the greater the potential flow of creative influence, the more irresistible the spark that ignites literary imaginations. Translation plays an inimitable, essential part in the expansion of literary horizons through multilingual fertilization. A worldwide community of writers would be inconceivable without it.

Goethe believed that a literature exhausts itself and its resources become vitiated if it closes itself off to the influences and contributions of other literatures. Not only literature but language itself thrives as it makes connections with other languages. The result of the linguistic infusion of new means of expression is an expansion of vocabulary, evocative potentiality, and structural experimentation. In other words, the broadening of horizons that comes with translation does not affect only readers, speakers, and writers of a language, but the very nature of the language itself. The more a language embraces infusions and transfusions of new elements and foreign turns of phrase, the larger, more forceful, and more flexible it becomes as an expressive medium. How sad to contemplate the efforts of know-nothing governments and exclusionary social movements to first invent and then foster the mythical "purity" of a language by barring the use of any others within a national territory. The language they wish to preserve would eventually be worn away, eroded and impoverished by a lack of access to new and unfamiliar means of expression and communication, if it were not for irresistible, inevitable surges of enriching intercultural and multilinguistic currents across the world.

At the center of discussions of books and literature is the reader, a figure frequently alluded to in broad generalities, although in that sense there is no reader, there are only readers, individuals who respond to a text in idiosyncratic, eccentric, and thoroughly unpredictable ways. By the same token, we probably should avoid this kind of unitary abstraction when referring en masse to writers, translators, publishers, and critics, but the temptation to do so is difficult to resist, especially when we engage in general discussions of the contemporary state of the book.

For those of us who take literature very seriously, picking up a work of fiction is the start of an adventure comparable in anticipatory excitement to what I imagine is felt by an athlete warming up for a competition, a mountain climber preparing for the ascent: it is the beginning of a process whose outcome is unknown, one that promises the thrill and elation of success but may as easily end in bitter disappointment. Committed readers realize at a certain point that literature is where we have learned a good part of the little we know about living. Certainly we learn from vital experience, but experience can be direct or vicarious, and the most wide-ranging, most profound kind of vicarious experience I know of is the one we encounter in works of literature. In English-language fiction, consider the obscure modes of behavior and unpredictable attitudes contained in the subtle revelations of Henry James or Edith Wharton, the stunning aperçus of Philip Roth, the bitterness of loss in Ernest Hemingway, the world-weary sophistication of Graham Greene, the dazzling experimentation and acute sensitivity to character of James Joyce or Virginia Woolf. Then remember the astonishment of the utterly alien and new that washed over you the first time you read a novel by Fyodor Dostoevsky or became aware of the extraordinary precision of Gustave Flaubert's observations, the profundity of Thomas Mann's sense of history and its not always loving embrace of individuals, the imaginative menace of José Saramago's hyperrealism, the piercing, ironic calamities of W. G. Sebald's chronicles. I never have forgotten my adolescent self discovering nineteenth-century Russian and French novelists: the world seemed to grow large, expanding like an unbreakable balloon; it became broader and deeper as I contemplated characters more diverse and unpredictable than anything I could have imagined on my own. Surely writers like Stendhal and Balzac, Gogol and Tolstoy, created entire galaxies in their writing. It is unthinkable, almost unbearable to contemplate the possibility of being deprived of those universes because one does not know French and Russian well enough to read their books.

Reading novels first in English and in translation, and later in Spanish (and occasionally in one or two other Romance languages), was how I confirmed for myself the actuality of the unforeseeable, the omnipresence of the unimaginable, the prevailing variance and dissimilarity that dominate human affairs, and then learned—or at least was exposed to—a handful of profoundly important ways to cope with the shifting ground. Over the years, as I have continued to explore the world of fiction, the kind of perception that grows out of and is nourished by reading keeps expanding until it spills over into ordinary, concrete life. Haven't you thought on more than one occasion that in a kind of authorial prescience on the part of some writers, or with a Borgesian creation of fictional realities within the confines of a physical, concrete actuality, certain scenes and conversations on the street, in restaurants, or on trains come right out of novels by Turgenev or Kafka or Grass? And haven't you realized with a start that whatever ways you may have devised for responding to those situations probably come from the same novels too?

Imagine how bereft we would be if the only fictional worlds we could explore, the only vicarious literary experiences we could have, were those written in languages we read easily. The deprivation would be indescribable. Depending on your linguistic accomplishments, this would mean you might never have the opportunity to read Homer or Sophocles or Sappho, Catullus or Virgil, Dante or Petrarch or Leopardi, Cervantes or Lope or Quevedo, Ronsard or Rabelais or Verlaine, Tolstoy or Chekhov, Goethe or Heine: even a cursory list of awe-inspiring writers is practically endless, though I have not even left western Europe or gone past the nineteenth century to compile it. Then try to imagine never experiencing any literature written in the countless other languages you may not know: in my case, these would include Polish, Czech, German, Hungarian, Bulgarian, Turkish, Russian, and all the myriad languages of the Middle East, Asia, and Africa. The mere idea creates a prospect that is intolerably, inconceivably bleak.

Putting to the side for a moment the dire state of publishing today or the lamentable tendency of too many publishers to treat translators cavalierly or dismiss them as irrelevant, the fact is that many readers tend to take translation so much for granted that it is no wonder translators are so frequently ignored. We seem to be a familiar part of the natural landscape—so customary and commonplace that we run the risk of becoming invisible. This may be why many university English departments often declare a monopoly on the teaching of what they choose to call world literature or humanities, putting together lists of readings that include a large number of works in translation. I cannot quarrel with the inclusion of translations on any reading list, yet in the process foreign-language departments and their teachers of literature, the ones with real expertise in the works studied, are effectively snubbed. I have never been able to find the logic or coherence in that. Is there someone on a curriculum committee somewhere who does not know or cannot tell the difference between works in English and works in translation? The best face I can put on it is that the ironic disconnect may be an academic trait.

Our world as dedicated readers depends on the availability of translated works, classical and contemporary, yet in English-speaking nations, major commercial publishers are strangely resistant to publishing them. The sad statistics indicate that in the United States and the United Kingdom, for example, only two to three percent of books published each year are literary translations. This is not the universal nature of the translating beast: in western Europe, in countries like France or Germany, Italy or Spain, and in Latin America, the number is anywhere from twenty-five to forty percent. I don't know how to account for this, but the recalcitrance of the English-language publishing industry seems unshakeable and immutable. For most houses, translated works are not of compelling interest regardless of the wider significance readers and writers may find in them. Frequently, in fact, translations are actively discouraged. They can be commercially successful (think of the cachet enjoyed in this country by *The Name of the Rose; Beowulf; Don Quixote;* anything by Roberto Bolaño), and still the majority of American and British publishers resist the very idea of translation and persistently hold the line against the presence of too many translated works in their catalogues. Some years ago, to my most profound consternation, I was told by a senior editor at a prestigious house that he could not even consider taking on another translation since he already had two on his list.

A persistent explanation for the phenomenon of translation resistance—at least, the one I have heard most often—is that English-language readers are put off by translations (the presumptive reason, incidentally, for publishers' longtime and forever-mindless reluctance to put the translator's name, in legible size, on the cover of a book that has been brought over into a second language). This is another of those publishing shibboleths presented as divine truth, but it really doesn't make sense to me. The market-driven publishing industry seems to be caught up in a chicken-and-egg conundrum: is a limited readership for translations the reason so few are published in the Anglophone world, or is that readership limited because English-language publishers provide their readers with so few translations, especially of works by younger writers in languages thought of as exotic (a term applied to languages from anywhere but western Europe). These amazing statistics regarding the embarrassingly low percentage of translations in the English-speaking world represent or express a new kind of iron curtain that we have constructed around ourselves, to our detriment and to the detriment of literature in general. I realize that the number of readers of literature is on the decline, and that serious, dedicated editors face real difficulties in bringing good books to the marketplace. It often seems, however, that translations and the people who create them can become too easy a target for a beleaguered industry, although shortchanging translators and ignoring translation in no way helps to solve the grave problem of a reduced readership.

Reviewers seem to care about translation even less than publishers do. I admit to a somewhat jaundiced attitude toward most book reviewers. In overwhelming numbers they tend not to speak substantively about translation or its practitioners, even when the book they are reviewing is a translated work. Their omissions and distortions are extraordinary, and certainly as wrongheaded as the publishers' pretense that the translator's name not only is of no importance but is likely to be a serious impediment to the success of the book. A very well-known figure in the literary world who regularly reviewed for an acclaimed periodical once defended the omission of any mention of the translation in his piece on a translated novel by stating that since he did not know the language of the original, there was nothing he can say about the translated version. By implication, he was actually saying that the purpose of any such discussion in a review is to perform an accuracy check, which is hardly the point, since any competent translator would already have made countless checks for accuracy before the book ever reached the publisher's hands.

Unlike many publications that do not even mention the translator's name, however, some apparently require their writers to indicate somewhere in the review that the book under consideration has been translated from another language, and with some few outstanding exceptions, this burdensome necessity is taken care of with a single dismissive and uninformative adverb paired with the verb "translated." This is the origin of that perennial favorite "ably," but I wonder how reviewers know even that much. It usually is clear from the review that, like the writer mentioned in the previous paragraph, most of them do not read the original language, and sometimes I doubt that they have even read the translation. This deadly shallowness leads me to ask: "ably" compared with what? By an act of prestidigitation that verges on the miraculous, however, they often discuss the style and language of the book as if they were discussing the language of the original writer, as if the work of the translator—the work they are reviewing—were not the connection that has allowed them to read the book in the first place. Remarkable, isn't it? Do they think translations consist of a magical kind of tracing paper placed over the original text? Are they really convinced that the contribution of the translator is a merely rote mechanical exercise on that miraculous tracing paper, like the wondrous interlinear translations of second-year language students?

Intrinsic to the concept of a translator's fidelity to the effect and impact of the original is making the second version of the work as close to the first writer's intention as possible. A good translator's devotion to that goal is unwavering. But what never should be forgotten or overlooked is the obvious fact that what we read in a translation is the translator's writing. The inspiration is the original work, certainly, and thoughtful literary translators approach that work with great deference and respect, but the execution of the book in another language is the task of the translator, and that work should be judged and evaluated on its own terms. Still, most reviewers do not acknowledge the fact of translation except in the most perfunctory way, and a significant majority seem incapable of shedding light on the value of the translation or on how it reflects or illuminates the original.

Even if it is unrealistic to wish that every reviewer of a translated work were at least bilingual, it is not unreasonable to require a substantive and intelligent acknowledgment of the reality of the translation. I am certainly not lamenting the fact that most reviewers do not make one-for-one lexical comparisons in order to point out whatever mistakes the translator may have made—a useless enterprise that enlightens no one since the book has already been published and errors cannot be rectified until the next printing—but I do regret very sincerely that so few of them have devised an intelligent way to review both the original and its translation within the space limitations imposed by the publication. It seems to me that their inability to do so is a product of intransigent dilettantism and tenacious amateurism, the menacing two-headed monster that runs rampant through the inhospitable landscape peopled by those who write reviews.

And so we come back to the first question: why does translation matter, and to whom? I believe it matters for the same reasons and in the same way that literature matters—because it is crucial to our sense of ourselves as humans. The artistic impulse and the need for art in our species will not be denied. It has been with us almost from the beginning of our history, and despite profound changes in culture, customs, and expectations, it remains with us all over the world in a variety of guises. Where literature exists, translation exists. Joined at the hip, they are absolutely inseparable and, in the long run, what happens to one happens to the other. Despite all the difficulties the two have faced, sometimes separately, usually together, they need and nurture each other, and their long-term relationship, often problematic but always illuminating, will surely continue for as long as they both shall live.

1 authors, translators, and readers today

Translation seen as conversation—
for conversation assumes equality
among the speakers—is clearly the
language of languages, the
language that all languages should
speak.

—NGUGI WA THIONG-O,
director, International Center for
Writing and Translation,
University of California at Irvine

The vast, constantly expanding sea of contemporary literature can easily swamp any reader interested in keeping abreast of new works and new writers. In my own case, and I believe this is true for many other people as well, I can find no way to read all the good books published in even one year in a single language. Despite our best intentions and finest desires, too many of those books pass us by as the pile of still-to-be-read volumes grows higher and higher, while our eyes seem to move more and more slowly, and our already jammed schedules become tighter and increasingly difficult to manage. This dire lack of time is extreme and appears to grow worse minute by minute, day by day. The inevitable next question is, I think, sadly obvious: why add to the welter of indispensable, high-priority titles we will never read by translating even more indispensable, high-priority titles from other languages? Our bookshelves already sag under the crushing weight of important volumes of contemporary writing. Fiction, poetry, history, biography, philosophy, memoir—how can we find the time to read even a small part of the significant works published in English each year in the United States and the United Kingdom?

It is true, of course, that despite some very amusing theorizing on the subject by the late Guatemalan satirist and fiction writer Augusto Monterroso in his far-too-brief "How I Got Rid of Five Hundred Books" (117–121), quantity is not, or certainly should not be, key to this discussion: people do not read books by the pound, or keep a competitive record of how many volumes they own, or have their intelligence and education judged, by themselves or by others, on the basis of the number of feet of book-filled shelving that lines their walls. But the reality is staggering: keeping up with what is originally published in English each year would mean, at the very least, that we would have to give up gainful employment, never see another movie or play, never attend another concert, and certainly never take another walk or have another leisurely meal with friends. And yet it is also true that the fundamentally judicious and logical question, along with its implicit answer, of why we should even bother to translate books that may very well go unopened by readers who are increasingly pressed for time (not to mention a depressingly large public that has no interest at all in reading for what some publications irritatingly term a "literary experience") needs to be countered with another, even more fundamental question: what do we forfeit, historically, potentially, and in actuality, as individuals and as a society, if we somehow lose access to translated literature by voluntarily reducing its presence in our community or passively watching and quietly standing by as its availability to us is drastically and arbitrarily curtailed?

To begin to formulate a response, and to put the issue as succinctly and undramatically as possible, the question probably should be rephrased: What is the point of translating books? Why does the translation of literature matter at all, and whom does it benefit? What is the purpose of promoting the art of literary translation with funded projects, symposia, international conferences, lecture series, professional organizations and journals, prizes, and the occasional residency? Where is the cultural profit, the public good? Perhaps a case could be made for supporting the translation of classic works of world literature (very few, even among the most cynical and audacious, would have the temerity to dispute the value of reading Homer or Dante or Cervantes or Shakespeare, regardless of one's native language, if one does not know Ancient Greek or Medieval Italian or Renaissance Spanish or English), but we have already posited an overabundance of new books to read in a single language. Aren't there more than enough contemporary works of fiction, poetry, and drama in English to satisfy anyone's literary predilections without our having to venture into the fearsome, reputedly money-losing, famously reader- and publisher-resistant terrain of translation?

For translators, of course, there can never be enough translations. But in a masterwork of startling intellectual flimflammery, there are some academics whose names, as Cervantes so beautifully put it, I do not care to remember, who actually believe that translations should be banned entirely from the curriculum of any self-respecting university. Either their beleaguered students of literature read the work in the original language, these pedagogues proclaim, or they don't read it at all, at least not in a class at the university. It is a stunning proposition, isn't it? Think of what it really means. If, for example, you do not read Akhmatova in Russian, Brecht in German, Montale in Italian, García Lorca in Spanish, Valéry in French, Kazantzakis in Greek, Ibsen in Norwegian, Strindberg in Swedish, Saramago in Portuguese, or Singer in Yiddish, you should not be permitted to study those authors in a formal, credit-bearing course on twentieth-century literature, especially if you are enrolled in graduate school. I spent a good part of my adult life teaching, usually in foreign-language departments, and although I wanted everyone in the world to study a few languages other than their own, the idea of eliminating translations entirely from the university course of study never once occurred to me. How could we get along without them? More to the point, how could I get along without them, when there are so many important languages in the world I cannot read and so many valuable works of literature I would be entirely ignorant of if they had not been translated into English?

And yet the niggling, distasteful question persists: really, what is the point of translating works of literature when we already have a huge surfeit of books in our own language and a diminishing number of readers? Suppose we narrow the inquiry and consider only the translation of fiction. Are matters simplified and made more intelligible if we set aside plays, poetry, short fiction, essays, and all other species of belles-lettres and attempt to justify and support the translation of contemporary novels on the presumption that this restriction might produce a more manageable number of translated books for indefatigable readers of English? No, not at all. Even in this limited sphere, no one can read every novel originally published in English in a year's time, let alone all the translated ones. Even though the number of novels brought over into English each year is pitifully, frighteningly small when compared with the number of translated novels produced in publication centers around the world, translations of fiction seem to add unconscionably to the burden of unopened volumes that weighs on every serious reader. Still, it must be said that this is not the real issue. The raw number of books that we as individuals can read in a period of twelve months, or even a lifetime, is a profoundly inconsequential, even trivial approach to the somber question that has been raised. Other considerations, with broader implications, seem much more relevant.

First, there is the disquieting matter of the growth and spread of an increasingly intense jingoistic parochialism in our country—the kind of attitude that leads certain people who should know better to believe that their nation and their language are situated, by a kind of divine right, at the center of the universe. The resulting self-image or self-conceptualization by definition transforms everyone else in the world into benighted barbarians whose cultures are unimportant and whose languages are insignificant. Certainly this is not, as we all realize, an exclusively modern phenomenon or one that is restricted to a particular language or nation, but we will focus on the situation most of us probably know best. In the United States, some speakers of English believe their native tongue is sanctified and therefore spiritually superior to any other. I am sure many of you have heard about and some may even have seen the bumper sticker, widely popular in those parts of our country where people have mounted impassioned crusades against bilingualism in any form, but especially Spanish/English bilingualism, which claims: "If English Was Good Enough For Jesus, It's Good Enough For Me." After the first incredulous giggle, this public display of ignorance verging on the lunatic brings more than one despairing tear to my eye. Surely Luis Rafael Sánchez, the Puerto Rican novelist and playwright, had something like this chauvinistic derangement in mind when, in his inimitably ironic way, he coined the term Essential Nation of the Universe as an alternative name for the United States of America in his latest book, *Indiscreciones de un perro gringo* (Indiscretions of a gringo dog), the fictional memoir of Buddy Clinton, regrettably killed in 2002 by a car in Chappaqua, New York.

The high degree of xenophobia rampant in our country may help explain the American reluctance to embrace translation, but in my experience, British publishers display the same lethal disinclination, exemplified not only in a professional, deepseated distrust of translation—they publish as woefully few literary translations in Great Britain as we do in the United States, a figure that hovers around three percent of all the books published in a year—but also in their widespread and highhanded tendency to harbor an unshakeable, insular contempt for American English. I have discovered, to my horror, that far too many British publishers insist on Anglicizing texts that have been translated by those of us who, to their minds, are little more than semiliterate American ex-colonials who flatter ourselves into thinking that the yawp we speak and write is actually English. In my impassioned objections to unreasonable editorial changes by publishers in Great Britain, I have said that in the past, when I as an American read books by D. H. Lawrence, James Joyce, or Virginia Woolf, I did not expect their language to sound exactly like Ernest Hemingway's, William Faulkner's, or John Steinbeck's; that I was not irretrievably confounded by differences in spelling or hopelessly discouraged or confused by unfamiliar words or turns of phrase or lexical references that were usually clarified by context; that anything not clarified by context was certainly easy enough to look up. My arguments did not move these publishers at all, not even when I appealed to nationalist sentiment and asked if they really believed that English readers were significantly more ignorant and unsophisticated than their American counterparts. How sorry I am now that I only recently learned of this remark, made by William Carlos Williams, in the 1957 folio *Poems in Folio:*

> I don't speak English, but the American idiom. I don't know how to write anything else, and I refuse to learn.

How happy I would have been to use the citation in an unapologetic verbal counterattack. I did, however, finally manage to persuade the more reasonable among the English publishers that they could feel free to alter spelling in my manuscripts to conform to British usage but that I absolutely had to have final approval of lexical changes. This arrangement is now part of my contract for any book I translate that is published, usually at roughly the same time, in both the United States and the United Kingdom.

Sadly, this peculiar conflict between national—or is it continental?—variants of the same language is not confined to English. It is sobering and instructive to realize that Latin American writers too have often faced a comparable high-handed disdain for their American language on the part of Spanish publishers. A notorious instance of this kind of editorial imperialism involves Gabriel García Márquez. In *Living to Tell the Tale,* he recounts the following anecdote about the 1962 publication in Spain of *La mala hora* (*In Evil Hour;* originally titled *Este pueblo de mierda*):

> Not content with touching up the grammar in the dialogues, the proofreader permitted himself to change the style with a heavy hand, and the book was filled with Madrilenian patches that had nothing to do with the original. As a consequence, I had no recourse but to withdraw my permission from the edition because I considered it adulterated, and to retrieve and burn the copies that had not yet been sold. The reply of those responsible was absolute silence. (232–233)

Oh, how familiar that lofty silence seems!

After he translated the book back into what he calls his Caribbean dialect, García Márquez sent the corrected manuscript to a Mexican publisher and brought out that revision as the first edition in 1966.

It is unfortunate that many American editors are not far behind their English and peninsular colleagues in bare-faced chauvinism and unforgivable, willful know-nothingness. I do not believe publishing houses here reciprocate or return the linguistic insult by going out of their way to Americanize the texts of books first published in the United Kingdom or those written by British authors, though it has been pointed out to me that many books are turned down in the United States because they are "too British." However, you may have read the January–February 2004 issue of the *Atlantic Monthly* in which Benjamin Schwarz, the book review editor, made this remarkable observation in a statement called "Why we review the books we do":

> We tend to focus on prose-style in our assessment of fiction. It's obviously far more difficult to do so when reviewing literature in translation, because both the reviewer and the reader of the book encounter not the author's writing but the translator's rendering of it. Hence we run fewer pieces on translated works.

Quite a few indignant responses, including mine, were sent to the magazine, but as far as I know, none were published. I'm afraid, however, that it did not occur to anyone to ask Schwarz if he really believed that the best way to deal with our remarkable paucity of vocabulary for reviewing or even talking about translated works was simply not to talk about them at all. One of the brightest students in a seminar I taught recently asked whether, in *The Autumn of the Patriarch,* we were reading Rabassa or García Márquez. My first, unthinking response was "Rabassa, of course," and then a beat later, I added, "and

García Márquez." The ensuing discussion of how difficult it is to separate the two, and what it meant to us as readers, writers, and critics to make the attempt, was one of the liveliest and most engrossing we had that semester. Among other things, it spoke directly to the core of how translated books should be reviewed.

It has been suggested to me by an academic friend who is not a translator but is an indefatigable critic, editor, and reader, that translation may well be an entirely separate genre, independent of poetry, fiction, or drama, and that the next great push in literary studies should probably be to conceptualize and formulate the missing critical vocabulary. That is to say, it is certainly possible that translations may tend to be overlooked or even disparaged by reviewers, critics, and editors because they simply do not know what to make of them, in theory or in actuality. In the event you think I am exaggerating the lack of rational, thoughtful discussion of translations for reasons of parochial interest or because I have eaten more than my share of sour grapes, I will cite in its entirety a paragraph from a May 2007 review in a British publication of my translation of Mayra Montero's *Dancing to "Almendra"*:

> Montero's story was originally written in Spanish but has been translated by Edith Grossman for English readers. Fortunately the translation doesn't seem to have taken anything away from the beautiful style in which the book is written.

There is no indication, of course, that the reviewer can read Spanish or that his or her judgment is based on a reasoned comparison of the two versions of the novel. There almost never is in the dismissive reviews I have seen of translated works—mine, and those of other translators as well. A rare exception to this kind of uninformed reviewer is James Wood, who consistently pays serious attention to the real value of translation, bringing into focus the question of how books under review are translated and what priorities seem to guide translators in their choices. An example of his approach to writing about translations is in the November 26, 2007, issue of the *New Yorker*, where Wood has a beautiful piece on the celebrated translation of *War and Peace* by Richard Pevear and Larissa Volokhonsky, published by Knopf. I'll cite a few sentences from this review to give you an idea of Wood's perspicacity in discussing the work, and the thoughtful attention to relevant detail that creates so telling a difference between him and too many other reviewers:

> Literary translators tend to divide into what one could call orig-
> inalists and activists. The former honor the original text's quid-
> dities, and strive to reproduce them as accurately as possible in the
> translated language; the latter are less concerned with literal ac-
> curacy than with the transposed musical appeal of the new work.
> Any decent translator must be a bit of both. . . . Translation is not
> a transfer of meaning from one language to another, Pevear writes,
> but a dialogue between two languages.

I am an indifferent historian and a worse theoretician, particularly when it comes to formal or theoretical literary and translation studies, but from time to time, when I contemplate the suspicion and resistance of the publishing establishment and its reviewing satellites toward translation, I wonder whether along with the lack of critical vocabulary, the difficulty may stem, at least in part, from a not-always-useful holdover of an earlier time. An unprecedented glorification of individualism and individual creativity held sway during the Romantic period, an emphatic celebration of a narrowly interpreted uniqueness and originality that is still extremely prominent in our thinking today. It is perfectly clear that by definition translators translate works written by someone else. Obviously we are not the first creators of the text, but I have the sense that at an earlier time in the history of the West—during the Renaissance, say—it never would have occurred to anyone to display contempt for the second writer or to feel any special ambivalence about the very concept of translation, particularly when the works in question had been brought over from classical and biblical languages.

Along these lines, Robert Wechsler cites Serge Gavronsky, the poet and translator from French:

> Readers always want—it's a Romantic preoccupation, never existed before the nineteenth century—authenticity. They somehow believe that if someone signs a text, that text was secreted by that

body. Cocteau has a lovely image: he says, "I shit my books." In a wonderful way, that's what readers want. They want to smell the feces of authenticity. So when a translator comes on, he appears to be an intercessor . . . because he didn't write it. (83)

During the Renaissance, however, there was a proliferation of works transposed into modern European tongues from Greek, Latin, and Hebrew, and as I mentioned earlier, the inescapable cultural fact of translation may well be the best overarching general description we have of that historical period. Here is what the translators of the King James version of the Bible, first published in 1611, had to say about their work. I would venture to add that their opinion of translation was the one commonly held at the time:

> Translation it is that openeth the window, to let in the light; that breaketh the shell, that we may eat the kernel; that putteth aside the curtain, that we may look into the most holy place; that removeth the cover of the well, that we may come by the water. (quoted in Wechsler, 11)

And even though Cervantes compared reading a translation to looking at a tapestry from the back, not once did he deny the inherent value of the enterprise. With typical irony, in fact, he lets us know that the entire first part of *Don Quixote* has been translated from Arabic, but then with the kind of double-edged mordancy that makes his sensibility so modern, Cervantes immediately throws doubt not only on the veracity and reliability of the translator but stresses as well the probable mendacity of the original author.

Can it be that our current rejection of translation grows out of an overweening and misguided admiration for Romantic concepts of innovation and creativity? Or does the real, essential explanation lie elsewhere? Factors I have mentioned briefly (the self-congratulatory ignorance of the bumper sticker, or the close-minded editorial policy of major British publishers, or the ineptitude of most reviewers of translated books, or the startling provincialism of an important American periodical) all speak to a deeply imprinted cultural dogmatism and linguistic isolationism that may constitute the primary obstacle to literary translation in the English-speaking world. I would like to further explore the social ramifications and political repercussions of this grim possibility.

In his introduction to *Words Without Borders,* Andre Dubus III comments on the glaring reality of our American parochialism:

> We are, of course, a country of immigrants. We come from the very cultures we no longer seem to know. A recent National Geographic study tested 18–24-year-old Americans, 83 percent of whom could not find Afghanistan on a map. 70 percent could not find Israel or Iran. Only 37 percent could locate Iraq. When asked the religion of India's majority population, nearly half answered Muslim when it is Hindu. A full 80 percent of Americans do not have passports, and there is this alarming statistic: . . . "50 percent

of all the books in translation now published world wide are translated from English, but only 6 percent are translated into English." Our own [former] president has publicly referred to Slovakia as "Slovenia," has called Kosovars "Kosovarians," Greeks "Grecians," and East Timorese "East Timorians." . . .

There are theories as to how we've become so ignorant of other cultures around the world: geography and foreign languages are no longer taught in schools; U.S. media companies have cut back on world news coverage; we are isolated between two oceans and have friendly neighbors to the north and south and can afford the luxury of being provincial. . . . The consequences are dire: we have never been less isolationist in the variety of goods and services we consume from around the world, and never have we been more ignorant of the people who produce them. This is, if nothing else, fertile territory for misunderstanding, unresolved conflict, and yes, war. (xi–xii)

The free, essential exchange of literary ideas, insights, and intuitions—a basic reciprocity of thought facilitated and enhanced by the translation of works from other cultures—is a decisively significant, even defining phenomenon. I think it reasonable to suggest that we can use the wide availability of and free access to translations in any society as a clear, determinative sign of vigorous, uncensored freedom of communication, an issue that deserves to be at the forefront of our political thinking. It is a compelling and original benchmark to consider in our continual, crucially important efforts to protect liberty.

I have already alluded to the essential importance of literary translation in the kind of civilized world we would like to inhabit, and touched briefly on the profound significance of a free-wheeling, ongoing exchange among languages and the literatures and cultures they express and contain, what Ngugi Wa Thiong-o, author of the epigraph to this chapter, calls their conversation and Richard Pevear their dialogue. By way of contrast, it is crucial for us to think carefully and clearly about the importance and weight that dictatorships all over the world attribute to language: to how it is used, and to what end, and by whom. Oppressive regimes have an incontestable penchant for dominating, corrupting, and stultifying language. Despotic governments are willing to go to extraordinary lengths in their usually successful, tragic official efforts to control, restrict, and narrow access to the spoken and written word. Imprisoned writers, banned books, censored media, restrictions on translations, even repeated attempts to abolish what are called "minority" languages (consider, as one example among many, the bitter struggle to eradicate Catalán during the long years of the Franco regime in Spain), are all clear indications that tyrannies take language, books, and access to information and ideas very seriously—much more seriously than democracies do. George Orwell's ghastly vision in *1984* of the creation of Newspeak and its intended consequence—the conscious perversion of thought processes in those who are exposed to impoverished language and diminished communication—is not, as we have come to realize, pure dystopian fiction but a reflection of tendencies toward oppression that already exist in our history-battered world, the proclivities toward subjugation that we ignore at our own peril and must resist wherever and whenever they appear.

It seems to me that the defense and furtherance of literary translation, in particular the translation into English of young authors writing in what are so dismissively termed "exotic languages," is—or should be—an intrinsic element in our commitment to free speech and civil liberty in this and other countries. I do not think that recognizing the interconnections among literature and translation, freedom and repression, the esthetic and the political, necessarily places an unconscionable ideological burden on the creation of works of art, or implies an imposition of unacceptable controls. I am speaking not of a writer's loyalties, intentions, or specific ideas but of our own society's willingness to embrace—at least give a hearing to—other attitudes and perspectives, other ways of looking at the world. This kind of reasoned approach to a broad range of diversified opinion represents a mode of thought that increasingly seems to be a wistful fantasy or a dream of the gleaming city on the hill, but I believe it can be defended, facilitated, and enhanced through the value we place on translation. As Ammiel Alcalay has said in his introduction to Miljenko Jergović's short story collection *Sarajevo Marlboro:*

The circuitous routes traveled by literary texts across various borders, checkpoints, blockades and holding pens should finally, once and for all, lay to rest the romantic notion that such texts announce themselves and arrive simply by virtue of their inherent qualities as literature. Nothing could be farther from the truth: like any commodity, literary texts gain access through channels and furrows that are prepared by other means. Fashion, chance encounters, fortuitous circumstances, surrogate functions, political alliances and cataclysmic events such as war or genocide are much more certain and constant catalysts than judgment based on actual literary history or cultural importance. The texts that manage to sneak through the policing of our monolingual borders still only provide a mere taste—fragmented, out of context—of what such works might represent in their own cultures. (vii)

In another lament for our tendency toward insularity and consequent self-imposed isolation, Lorraine Adams, in a piece in the January 6, 2008, *Book Review* of the *New York Times,* mentions what she calls the "burka effect"—the paucity of contemporary literature by Muslims that has been translated into English and which is therefore unavailable to many of us in the United States. As Adams says:

Literature in translation, regardless of its origin, has trouble finding American publishers. The languages of Islam, unlike European languages, particularly French and Spanish, are not often spoken or read by American editors. "When you have a book proposal, you have to have at least two chapters and a synopsis in English," explained Nahid Mozaffari, an Iranian historian who edited *Strange Times, My Dear,* a 2005 PEN anthology of contemporary Iranian literature. "But there's no money to pay for translation. A lot of what's happening is [that] nostalgic exiles or academics . . . [are] doing the chapter and synopsis in their spare time. Not all of them are good writers, and a lot [of literature] has been killed by bad translation."

The inferences that can be drawn from this kind of circumstance are extremely grave. The phenomenon means that we have been denied—or are choosing to deny ourselves—access to the writing of a large and significant portion of the world, including movements and societies that loom on our national horizon with potentially dreadful political implications made even more menacing by our general lack of familiarity with them. Wishful thinking has very little effect on reality. The fact that we stubbornly and willfully insist on remaining ignorant of a certain culture and its literature does not make that civilization cease to exist.

Yet English once held its arms wide to embrace other nations and languages, and in terms of lexicon, we still have extremely porous boundaries, taking in and welcoming vocabulary from all over the world. I have heard this phenomenon explained as the result of England's never having had an academy of the language to restrict and censor the presence of foreign elements and maintain at any cost the alleged "purity" of the mother tongue. The subject is an interesting chapter in the history of Europe, but whatever the etiology of the linguistic openness of

English, the clear consequence is the sheer vibrancy and flexibility of the language and its huge, constantly expanding, wonderfully contaminated, utterly impure lexicon. One example of this acceptance, ingestion, and domestication of the alien and strange was described in a November 8, 2007, interview in the *New York Times* with Daniel Cassidy, the author of *How the Irish Invented Slang*. The quantity of slang that has made its way into American English by way of the Gaelic-speaking Irish immigrants in New York is extraordinary. A pared-down list of lexical items etymologically rooted in Gaelic—"a back-room language, whispered in kitchens and spoken in the saloons," according to Cassidy—includes the words *doozy, hokum, jerk, punk, grifter, helter-skelter, slob, slum,* and *knack*. Even certain phrases such as "gee whiz," "holy cow," and "holy mackerel" are, Cassidy claims, Anglicized versions of Irish; I was especially taken by "Say uncle!" whose origin Cassidy traces to the Gaelic *anacal,* which translates into English as "mercy."

In the introduction I discussed a good number of reasons for fostering and promoting the translation of other literatures into English. I hope the benefit to us as readers is apparent by now. The importance to translators is self-evident. For contemporary writers, the positive effects and advantages are huge. To begin with, there is the ingrained desire of authors to reach as many readers as possible, and clearly the writer's audience expands as the book is translated and more and more people are able to read it. The English-language market not only is immense but, as I indicated earlier, it is also generally located in areas where the population tends to be literate and prosperous enough to purchase books. I have already alluded to the notion regarding the importance of a body of work being translated into English before a writer can even be considered for the Nobel Prize, since it is claimed, perhaps with reason, that English is the only language all the judges read. At the same time, however, the permanent secretary of the Swedish Academy, Horace Engdahl, in a widely reported statement to the press in October 2008, said that "Europe is still the center of the literary world. . . . The U.S. is too isolated, too insular. They don't translate enough and don't really participate in the big dialogue of literature."

Another salient reality that affects writers profoundly is the need for books to be translated into English in order for them to be brought over into other, non-European idioms, for English often serves as the linguistic bridge for translation into a number of languages. The translation of texts originally written in other Western languages into the enormous potential market represented by Chinese, for instance, often requires an English version first. Because, at least until recently, many more Chinese translators work from English than from Spanish, a considerable number of Chinese-language versions of Latin American literary works have actually been based on the English translations. Some years ago, French was the conduit language, and many Spanish-language versions of Russian books were actually rooted in French translations of the texts. Of equal significance is the possible transfer of the book into other media like film and television. Powerful filmmakers and television producers whose work is distributed worldwide are all apt to read English.

In brief, then, there seems to be overwhelming evidence to the effect that if you wish to earn a living as a writer, your works must be translated into English regardless of your native language. All these considerations mean that the impact on writers around the world of the current reluctance of English-language publishers to bring out translations can be dire, especially for younger authors. And no matter how patently naïve it may sound, I believe that, regardless of which bloated international conglomerate owns them, publishing houses in the United States and the United Kingdom have an ethical and cultural responsibility to foster literature in translation. I do not expect this to happen to a significant extent any time soon, but it is a goal worth supporting, and every once in a great while, to use the language of an earlier time, another editor's consciousness may in fact be raised, allowing him or her to join the small band of brave, committed souls in the industry who promote translated literature.

It well may be that in the best of all possible worlds—the one that antedates our Babelian hubris—all humans were able to communicate with all other humans, and the function of translators quite literally was unthinkable. But here we are in a world whose shrinking store of languages still comes to several thousand, a world where both isolationism and rampaging nationalism are on the rise and countries have begun to erect actual as well as metaphorical walls around themselves. I do not believe I am overstating the case if I say that translation can be, for readers as well as writers, one of the ways past a menacing babble of incomprehensible tongues and closed frontiers into the possibility of mutual comprehension. It is not a possibility we can safely turn our backs on.

2 translating cervantes

It's impossible to say a thing
exactly the way it was, because
what you say can never be exact,
you always have to leave
something out, there are too many
parts, sides, crosscurrents,
nuances; too many gestures,
which could mean this or that,
too many shapes which can never
be fully described, too many
flavors, in the air or on the
tongue, half-colors, too many.

—MARGARET ATWOOD,
The Handmaid's Tale

Translation is a strange craft, generally appreciated by writers (with a few glaring exceptions, like Milan Kundera, whose attack on his French translator was so virulent it achieved a sour kind of notoriety), undervalued by publishers (translators' fees tend to be so low that agents generally are not interested in representing them), trivialized by the academic world (there are still promotion and tenure committees that do not consider translations to be serious publications), and practically ignored by reviewers (astonishingly, it is still possible to find reviews that do not even mention the translator's name, let alone discuss the quality of the translation). It is an occupation that many critics agree is impossible at best, a betrayal at worst, and on the average probably not much more than the accumulated result of a diligent, even slavish familiarity with dictionaries, although bringing a text over into another language has a long and glorious history. It can boast of illustrious practitioners ranging from Saint Jerome to the translators at the court of King James to Charles Baudelaire to Ezra Pound, and as I indicated earlier, it is undeniably one of the characteristic, defining activities of the European Renaissance. As Robert Wechsler tells us in *Performing Without a Stage:*

> Translators could be much more clearly artists at a time when their role was the same as the author's: to entertain, to express, to expand their art and their language. Translation in Renaissance Europe was not a palliative for the disease of monoglotism, as it is today; it was a part of literature, a part of the passing of literary traditions and creations from language to language, and a part of the often conscious creation of modern vernacular languages that was central to the cause of the Reformation, religiously and politically. (69)

But you have all heard the mock definition, and may even have repeated it once or twice: Robert Frost allegedly defined poetry as the thing that gets lost in translation, an observation as devastating—and, I believe, as false—as the thundering Italian accusation, made respectable by age but for no other reason that I can think of, that all translators are traitors (*traduttore è traditore*).

If one disavows the proposition that professional translators are acutely and incurably pathological, the obvious question is why any sane person would engage in a much-maligned activity that is often either discounted as menial hackwork or reviled as nothing short of criminal. Certainly, for most of us who do, neither fame nor fortune is a serious motivation for so underpaid and undersung an enterprise. Something joyous and remarkable and intrinsically valuable in the work must move us to undertake it, for I can think of no other profession whose practitioners find themselves endlessly challenged to prove to the world that what they do is decent, honorable, and, most of all, possible. Over and over again, at conferences and in interviews, we are compelled to insist on what is hideously referred to as the "translatability" of literature, called on to assert the plausibility and value of translation, challenged to defend our very presence as the intermediary voice between the first author and the readers of the second version of the work—that is, the translation. As Clifford Landers of the American Translators Association once said, many reviewers write as if the English text had somehow sprung into existence independently. What these same reviewers do would be iniquitous if it did not have its own kind of lunatic humor: they are fond of quoting from the translated text in order to praise the author's style without once mentioning the fact that what they are citing is the translator's writing—unless, of course, they do not like the book or the author's style, and then the blame is placed squarely on the shoulders of the translator.

As I stated previously, "seamless" (or its comrade-in-arms "able") is probably the highest praise most translations can receive from most critics, who are chary with adjectives—or words of any kind, for that matter—when it comes to describing the work of a translator. Let me give you an admittedly acerbic translation of the damnation concealed in their faint praise: *able* is valued because it is a short word that takes up very little room when space is at a premium; *seamless,* I believe, actually refers to the properly humbled and chastised state of invisibility into which a translator mercifully chooses to disappear; "mercifully," because although translation is grudgingly admitted to be an unfortunate, regrettable necessity that may even be crucial to the transmission and communication of culture (sadly, not even the most gifted and exceptional students of languages can read every written language that has ever existed in the world), translators are expected to self-destruct as if we were personally responsible for the tower that caused the confusion of tongues for our species. One must always take the work seriously, never oneself, but that kind of humility smacks of a superficially subservient Uriah Heep insisting far too often on the unassuming servility of his character as he rubs his hands, rounds his shoulders, and formulates his criminal, devious plans.

How, then, are we to speak with intelligence, insight, and discernment of translation and its practitioners?

In an essay called "The Misery and the Splendor of Translation," the Spanish philosopher José Ortega y Gasset called translation a utopian enterprise, but, he said, so too is any human undertaking, even the effort to communicate with another human being in the same language. According to Ortega, however, the fact that they are utopian and may never be fully realized does not lessen the luminous value of our attempts to translate or to communicate: "Human tasks are unrealizable. The destiny of Man—his privilege and honor—is never to achieve what he proposes, and to remain merely an intention, a living utopia. He is always marching toward failure, and even before entering the fray he already carries a wound in his temple" (94). In translation, the ongoing, absolutely utopian ideal is fidelity. But fidelity should never be confused with literalness. Literalism is a clumsy, unhelpful concept that radically skews and oversimplifies the complicated relationship between a translation and an original.

The languages we speak and write are too sprawling and too unruly to be successfully contained. Despite the best efforts of prescriptive entities ranging from teachers of developmental composition insisting on proper style, good grammar, and correct punctuation, to the French government resolutely attempting to control and ultimately reduce the words and phrases imported into the national speech, living languages will not be regulated. They overflow even the most modern and allegedly complete dictionaries, which on publication are usually at least twenty years out of date; they sneer at restriction and correction and the imposition of appropriate or tasteful usage, and they revel in local slang, ambiguous meaning, and faddish variation. Like surly adolescents, they push against limits imposed by an academic or sociopolitical world they never made, and are in a state of perpetual rebellion. They are clearly more than accumulations of discrete lexical items, suitable formulations, or acceptable syntax, and the impact of their words is variable, multifaceted, and resonant with innumerable connotations that go far beyond first, or even fourth and fifth, dictionary definitions.

A single language, then, is slippery, paradoxical, ambivalent, explosive. When one tries to grasp it long enough to create a translation, the Byzantine complexity of the enterprise is heightened and intensified to an alarming, almost schizophrenic degree, for the second language is just as elusive, just as dynamic, and just as recalcitrant as the first. The experience of plunging into the maelstrom of signification and intention that whirls and boils between them as we attempt to transfer meaning between two languages, to hear the effects, the rhythms, the artfulness of both simultaneously, can verge on the hallucinatory.

Languages, even first cousins like Spanish and Italian, trail immense, individual histories behind them, and with all their volatile accretions of tradition, culture, and forms and levels of discourse, no two ever dovetail perfectly or occupy the same space at the same time. They can be linked by translation, as a photograph can link movement and stasis, but it is disingenuous to assume that translation, or photography for that matter, are representational, imitative arts in any narrow sense of the term.

Fidelity is the noble purpose, the utopian ideal, of the literary translator, but let me repeat: faithfulness has little to do with what is called literal meaning. If it did, the only relevant criterion for judging our work would be a mechanistic and naïve one-for-one matching of individual elements across two disparate language systems. This kind of robotic pairing does exist and is scornfully mocked as "translatorese," the misbegotten, unfaithful, and often unintentionally comic invention that exists only in the mind of a failed translator and has no reality in any linguistic universe. A wonderful depiction of this misshapen idiom can be found in one of my favorite cartoons, in which a bewildered translator asks a disgruntled author, "Do you not be happy with me as the translator of the books of you?"

If translators do not match up a series of individual elements and simply bring over words from one language to another, using that legendary linguistic tracing paper, then what do translators translate, and what exactly are they faithful to? Before I continue, I want to underscore a self-evident point: of course translators scour the dictionary, many dictionaries in fact, and rummage diligently, sometimes frantically, through thesauruses, and encyclopedias, and histories as well, for definitions and meanings. But this kind of lexical search and research, accompanied by many consultations with infinitely patient friends who are native speakers of the first language, and preferably are from the same region as the first author, is a preliminary activity associated with the rough draft, the initial step in a long series of revisions. Completing this preliminary stage is surely a sign of basic competence, but it is not central to the most important and challenging purposes of translation.

What I am about to say now directly contradicts Vladimir Nabokov's literalist theories of what a good translation should be, concretized in his practically unreadable English version of *Eugene Onegin* (127–143). I believe Nabokov was a brilliant novelist but a dismal translator: his notion of literal correspondences between languages—a surprisingly pedantic posture for so energetic, accomplished, and adventurous a writer—seems to me like something one might find down a rabbit hole or on the other side of a looking glass. One need only consider the plodding opening to his version of the novel in verse that is a monument of Russian literature:

> My uncle has most honest principles:
> when taken ill in earnest,
> he has made one respect him
> and nothing better could invent.
> To others his example is a lesson;
> but, good God, what a bore
> to sit by a sick man both day and night,
> without moving a step away!

To my mind, a translator's fidelity is not to lexical pairings but to context—the implications and echoes of the first author's tone, intention, and level of discourse. Good translations are good because they are faithful to this contextual significance. They are not necessarily faithful to words or syntax, which are peculiar to specific languages and can rarely be brought over directly in any misguided and inevitably muddled effort to somehow replicate the original. This is the literalist trap, because words do not *mean* in isolation. Words *mean* as indispensable parts of a contextual whole that includes the emotional tone and impact, the literary antecedents, the connotative nimbus as well as the denotations of each statement. I believe—if I didn't, I could not do the work—that the meaning of a passage can almost always be rendered faithfully in a second language, but its words, taken as separate entities, can almost never be. Translators translate context. We use analogy to re-create significance, searching for the phrasing and style in the second language which *mean* in the same way and *sound* in the same way to the reader of that second language. And this requires all our sensibility and as much sensitivity as we can summon to the workings and nuances of the language we translate into.

To balance the clear presumption of my criticizing Nabokov's theories of translation, I would like to cite John Dryden. In the preface to his translation of Ovid's *Epistles,* published in 1680, Dryden called literal translations "servile," and then, in his conclusion, he articulated, in perfectly eloquent language, his surprisingly modern approach to the issue of the translator's obligations:

> A translator that would write with any force or spirit of an original must never dwell on the words of his author. He ought to possess himself entirely and perfectly comprehend the genius and sense of his author, the nature of the subject, and the terms of the art or subject treated of. And then he will express himself as justly, and with as much life, as if he wrote an original: whereas he who copies word for word loses all the spirit in the tedious transfusion. (31)

Some time ago, when Gregory Rabassa was translating García Márquez's *One Hundred Years of Solitude,* he was asked by an exceptionally unintelligent interviewer whether he knew enough Spanish to translate the novel. Rabassa's glorious response was that this was certainly the wrong question. The real question, he said, was whether he knew enough English to do justice to that extraordinary book. I am not sure how the benighted interviewer replied: one hopes with stunned silence.

According to Ben Belitt, the important American translator and poet, Jorge Luis Borges had some extremely personal and very eccentric ideas about how he should be translated into English, his grandmother's native language. As cited in Wechsler's book, Belitt recounts:

> If Borges had had his way—and he generally did—all polysyllables would have been replaced [in English translation] by monosylla-

bles. . . . People concerned about the legitimacy of the literal might well be scandalized by his mania for dehispanization. "Simplify me. Modify me. Make me stark. My language often embarrasses me. It's too youthful, too Latinate. . . . I want the power of Cynewulf, Beowulf, Bede. Make me macho and gaucho and skinny." (101)

Borges also reportedly told his translator not to write what he said but what he meant to say. How can any translator ever accomplish what Borges requested? Isn't that the province of gifted psychics or literary critics? Yes on both counts, but I'll address only the issue of the second group.

By now it is a commonplace, at least in translating circles, to assert that the translator is the most penetrating reader and critic a work can have. The very nature of what we do requires that kind of deep involvement in the text. Our efforts to translate both denotation and connotation, to transfer significance as well as context, means that we must engage in extensive textual excavation and bring to bear everything we know, feel, and intuit about the two languages and their literatures. Translating by analogy means we have to probe into layers of purpose and implication, weigh and consider each element within its literary milieu and stylistic environment, then make the great leap of faith into the inventive rewriting of both text and context in alien terms. And this kind of close critical reading is sheer pleasure for shameless literature addicts like me, who believe that the sum of a fine piece of writing is more than its parts and larger than the individual words that constitute it. I have spent much of my professional life, not to mention all those years in graduate school, committed to the dual proposition that in literature, as in other forms of artistic expression, something more lurks behind mere surface, and that my purpose and role in life was to try to discover and interpret it, even if the goal turned out to be utopian in the sense suggested by Ortega y Gasset. I think this kind of longing to unravel esthetic mysteries lies at the heart of the study of literature. It surely is the essence of interpretation, of exegesis, of criticism, and of translation.

Yet now I feel obliged to confess that I am still mystified by the process of dealing with the same text in two languages, and have searched in vain for a way to express the bewildering relationship between translation and original, a paradoxical connection that probably can be evoked only metaphorically. The question that lurks in the corners of my mind as I work and revise and mutter curses at any fool who thinks the second version of a text is not an original, too, is this: what exactly am I writing when I write a translation? Is it an imitation, a reflection, a transposition, or something else entirely? In what language does the text really exist, and what is my connection to it? I do not mean to suggest that a translation is created with no reference to an original—that it is not actually a version of another text—but it seems clear that a translated work does have an existence separate from and different from the first text, if only because it is written in another language.

I do not have a grand, revelatory solution to the puzzle, even though essays like this one make an attempt to resolve the conundrum, but I think authors must often ask themselves the same question that is so difficult to articulate, must often see themselves as transmitters rather than creators of texts. The figure of the muse as an inspiring presence is ubiquitous and universal, testifying to the truth of the metaphor. I have often wondered why something as profoundly personal as creating literature should be seen so often as ultimately inspired by an "other," an external figure, perhaps an "original," and I have been intrigued by the idea that literary language may, in fact, be a form of translation. And here I mean translation not as the weary journeyman of the publishing world but as a living bridge between two realms of discourse, two realms of experience, and two sets of readers.

Octavio Paz, the Nobel Prize–winning Mexican writer, begins his essay "Translation: Literature and Letters" with the sentence: "When we learn to speak, we are learning to translate" (152). He states that children translate the unknown into a language that slowly becomes familiar to them, and that all of us are continually engaged in the translation of thoughts into language. Then he develops an even more suggestive notion: no written or spoken text is "original" at all, since language, what-ever else it may be, is a translation of the nonverbal world, and each linguistic sign and phrase translates another sign and phrase. And this means, in an absolutely utopian sense, that the most human of phenomena—the acquisition and use of lan-guage—is, according to Paz, actually an ongoing, endless pro-cess of translation; and by extension, the most creative use of language—that is, literature—is also a process of translation: not the transmutation of the text into another language but the transformation and concretization of the content of the writer's imagination into a literary artifact. As many observers, includ-ing John Felstiner and Yves Bonnefoy, have suggested, the translator who struggles to re-create a writer's words in the words of a foreign language in fact continues the original strug-gle of the writer to transpose nonverbal realities into language. In short, as they move from the workings of the imagination to the written word, authors engage in a process that is parallel to what translators do as we move from one language to another.

If writing literature is a transfer or transcription of internal experience and imaginative states into the external world, then even when authors and readers speak the same language, writ-ers are obliged to translate, to engage in the immense, utopian effort to transform the images and ideas flowing through their most intimate spaces into material, legible terms to which readers have access. And if this is so, the doubts and paradoxical questions that pursue translators must also arise for authors: Is their text an inevitable betrayal of the imagination and the creative impulse? Is what they do even possible? Can the written work ever be a perfect fit with that imaginative, creative original when two different languages, two realms of experience, can only approximate each other?

To follow and expand on the terms of this analogy, a literary text can be thought of as written in what is called, clumsily enough, the translation language, or target language, even though it is presented to readers as if it were written in the original, or source language. If the work is successful, it is read as "seamless" (the description that strikes terror in the hearts of all translators), but here the word means that when readers hold the work of literature in their hands, it has at last cut free and begun a life independent of the original—independent, that is, of the simultaneous internal states, the concurrent acts of imagination that initiate the writer's creative process. Language as the external artifact created by the writer needs metaphor to express the same internal states and acts of imagination that inspire the work, yet always looming in the background of all literary endeavor, establishing a gloomy, compelling counterpoint to the utopian model, is Flaubert's melancholy observation: "Language is like a cracked kettle on which we beat out tunes for bears to dance to, while all the time we long to move the stars to pity."

These kinds of considerations and speculations and problematic questions are always in my mind whenever I think about translation, especially when I am actually engaged in bringing a work of literature over into English. They certainly occupied a vast amount of mental space when I agreed to take on the immense task of translating *Don Quixote,* but only after I had repeatedly asked the publisher whether he was certain he had called the right Grossman, because my work as a translator had been focused on contemporary Latin American writers, not giants of the Renaissance in Spain. Much to my joy, he assured me that in fact I was the Grossman he wanted, and so my intimate, translatorial connection to the great novel began.

But there was more: hovering over me were dark sui generis clouds of intense trepidation, vast areas of apprehension and disquiet peculiar to this project. You can probably imagine what they were (just think what it would mean to an English-Spanish translator to take on the work of Shakespeare), but I will try to clarify a few of them for you.

There were the centuries of Cervantean scholarship, the specialized studies, the meticulous research, the untold numbers of books, monographs, articles, and scholarly editions devoted to this fiction-defining novel and its groundbreaking creator. Was it my obligation to read and reread all of these publications before embarking on the translation? A lifetime would not be enough time to do this scholarly tradition justice, I was no longer a young woman, and I had a two-year contract with the publisher.

There were other translations into English—at least twenty, by someone's count—a few of them recent and others, like Tobias Smollett's eighteenth-century version, considered classics in their own right. Was it my professional duty to study all of them? Before I took on the project, I recalled having read *Don Quixote* at least ten times, as a student and as a teacher, but always in Spanish except for my first encounter with the novel, in Samuel Putnam's 1948 translation, when I was a teenager. I had read no other translations since then. Was I willing to delay the work by years to give myself time to read each English-language version with care? To what end? Did I really want to fill my mind with the echoes of other translators' perceptions and interpretations?

Then there was the question of temporal distance, a chasm of four centuries separating me from Cervantes and the world in which he composed his extraordinary novel. I had translated complex and difficult texts before, some of them exceptionally obscure and challenging, in fact, but they were all modern works by living writers. Would I be able to transfer my contemporary experience as a translator to the past and feel some measure of ease as I brought the Spanish of the seventeenth century over into the English of the twenty-first? As a student I had spent a good number of years studying the prose writers and poets of the Spanish Golden Age, Cervantes among them, with some of the most erudite specialists in the field, including Joaquín Casalduero, Otis Green, Antonio Rodríguez Moñino, and José Montesinos, but was this sufficient preparation for undertaking the translation of a book that has the hallowed stature of a sacred text? Would my efforts—my incursions into the sacrosanct—amount to blasphemy?

What was I to do about the inevitable lexical difficulties and obscure passages? These occur in prodigious numbers in contemporary works and were bound to reach astronomical proportions in a work that is four hundred years old. As I've said, normally when I translate I dig through countless dictionaries and other kinds of references—most recently Google—for the meaning of words I don't know, and then my usual practice is to talk with those kind, patient, and generous friends who are from the same country as the author, and preferably from the same region within the country. As a last step in my lexical searches, I generally consult with the original writer, not for the translation of a word or phrase but for clarification of his or her intention and meaning. But *Don Quixote* clearly was a different matter: none of my friends came from the Spain of the early seventeenth century, and short of channeling, I had no way to consult with Cervantes. I was, I told myself in a tremulous voice, fervently wishing it were otherwise, completely on my own.

Two things came to my immediate rescue: the first was Martín de Riquer's informative notes in the Spanish edition of the book I used for the translation (I told García Márquez, whose *Living to Tell the Tale* I worked on immediately after *Don Quixote,* that Cervantes was easier to translate than he was because at least in a text by Cervantes there were notes at the bottom of the page). Riquer's editorial comments shed light on countless historical, geographical, literary, and mythical references, which I think tend to be more obscure for a modern reader than individual lexical items. Throughout his edition, Riquer takes on particularly problematic words by comparing their renderings in the earliest translations of *Don Quixote* into English, French, and Italian, and I have always found this—one language helping to explicate another—especially illuminating. The second piece of invaluable assistance came from an old friend, the Mexican writer Homero Aridjis, who sent me a photocopy of a dictionary he had found in Holland when he was a diplomat there: a seventeenth-century Spanish-English dictionary first published by a certain gentleman named Percivale, then enlarged by a professor of languages named Minsheu, and printed in London in 1623. The dictionary was immensely helpful at those dreadful times when a word was not to be found in María Moliner, or in the dictionary of the Real Academia, or in Simon and Schuster, Larousse, Collins, or Williams. I do not mean to suggest that there were no excruciatingly obscure or archaic phrases in *Don Quixote*—it has a lifetime supply of those—but despite all the difficulties I was fascinated to realize how constant and steady Spanish has remained over the centuries (as compared with English, for example), which meant that I could often use contemporary wordbooks to help shed light on a seventeenth-century text.

I wondered, too, if the novel would open to me as contemporary works sometimes do, and permit me to immerse myself in the intricacies of its language and intention. Would I be able to catch at least a glimpse of Cervantes' mind as I listened to his prose and began to live with his characters, and would I be able to keep that image intact as I searched for equivalent voices in English? On occasion, at a certain point in the translation of a book, I have been lucky enough to hit the sweet spot, when I can begin to imagine that the author and I have started to speak together—never in unison, certainly, but in a kind of satisfying harmony. In those instances it seems as if I can hear the author's voice in my mind speaking in Spanish at the same time that I manage to find a way to speak the work in English. The experience is exhilarating, symbiotic, certainly metaphorical, and absolutely crucial if I am to do what I am supposed to do—somehow get into the author's head and behind the author's eyes and re-create in English the writer's linguistic perceptions of the world.

And here I must repeat Ralph Manheim's observation comparing the translator to an actor who speaks as the author would if the author could speak English. A difficult role, and arduous enough with contemporary writers. What would happen to my performance when I began to interpret the work of an author who wrote in the seventeenth century—and not just an ordinary author but the remarkable man who is one of a handful of splendid writers who have determined the course of literature in the Western tradition? Despite all my years of study, I am not a Golden Age specialist: would I be able to play the Cervantean part and speak those memorable lines, or would the entire quixotic enterprise close down on its first night out of town, before it ever got to Broadway? Would I, in short, be able to write passages that would afford English-language readers access to this marvelous novel, allow them to experience the text in a way that approaches how readers in Spanish experience it now, and how readers experienced it four hundred years ago?

These were some of the fears that plagued me as I prepared to take on the project, but the prospect was not entirely bleak, dire, and menacing, of course. The idea of working on *Don Quixote* was one of the most exciting things that had happened to me as a translator. It was a privilege, an honor, and a glorious opportunity—thrilling, overwhelming, and terrifying. At this point I had the exchange with Julián Ríos that I mention in my translator's note to *Don Quixote.* I told Julián about the project, and about the apprehension I felt, and he told me not to be afraid because, he said, Cervantes was our most modern writer. All I had to do, according to Julián, was translate Cervantes the way I translated everyone else, meaning the contemporary authors whose works—Ríos's included—I had brought over into English. As I said in the note, this was "a revelation; it desacralized the project and allowed me, finally, to confront the text and find the voice in English"—in other words, Julián's comments permitted me to begin the process of translation (xvii–xx). In the back of my mind was the rather fanciful notion that if I could successfully translate the opening phrase— probably the most famous words in Spanish, comparable to the opening lines of Hamlet's "To be, or not to be" soliloquy in English, or, in Italian, the inscription over the gate to hell envisioned by Dante in the *Commedia,* and known even to people who have not read the entire work—then the rest of the novel would somehow fall into place. The first part of the sentence in Spanish reads: "En un lugar de la Mancha, de cuyo nombre no quiero acordarme . . . " I recited those words to myself as if they were a mantra, until an English phrase materialized that seemed to have a comparable rhythm and drive, that played with the multiple meanings of the word *lugar* (both "place" and "village"), and that echoed some of the sound of the original: "Somewhere in La Mancha, in a place whose name I do not care to remember . . . " It felt right to me, and with a rush of euphoric satisfaction I told myself I might actually be able to translate this grand masterpiece of a book.

Another major consideration was the question of which edition of *Don Quixote* to use for the translation. As with any classic work, there are many beautiful and valuable editions of the book; despite the mean-spirited speculation of one reviewer, whose name I do not care to remember, I did know about the highly acclaimed recent edition by Francisco Rico, but as I have already indicated, for reasons both critical and sentimental I decided to use Martín de Riquer's earlier one. Based on the first printing of the book, it includes all the oversights, lapses, and slips in Part One that Cervantes subsequently tried to correct, and to which he refers in Part Two, published ten years later. I have always loved the errors in the first printing and been charmed by the companionable feeling toward Cervantes that they create in me. Someone—one of the book's translators, I think—called *Don Quixote* the most careless masterwork ever written, and I thought it would be a shame if my translation lost or smoothed over or scholarshiped away that enthusiastic, ebullient quality, what I think of as the creative surge that allowed Cervantes to make those all-too-human mistakes and still write his crucially important and utterly original book. I am not suggesting, by the way, that Cervantes was a primitive savant or a man not fully conscious of the ramifications and implications of his art. He was, however, harried, financially hard-pressed, and overworked. Conventional wisdom informs us that even Homer nodded, and as every writer knows, in the urgency of getting a book into print, the strangest mistakes appear in the oddest places.

I decided, too, that I was not creating a scholarly work or an academic book, and therefore I would not study and compare editions—no more than I would begin my work by checking on how other translators had done theirs. And yet, despite my lack of academic intention, pretension, and purpose, for the first time in my translating career I chose to use footnotes, many of them based on the notes in Riquer's edition, and the others the result of my seemingly endless perusals of encyclopedias, dictionaries, and histories. These notes, which I wanted to be as unobtrusive and helpful as possible, were not meant as records or proofs of scholarly research but as clarifications for the reader of possibly obscure references and allusions—the kinds of clarifications made necessary in a contemporary version of the novel by external factors such as the passage of time, changes in education, transformations in the reading public, and the cultural differences between the United States in the twenty-first century and Spain in the seventeenth. There was no reason I could think of for an intelligent modern reader to be put off by difficulties in the text that were not intended by the author. For instance, the ballads or romances cited so frequently in *Don Quixote* by the characters and by Cervantes himself in the guise of the narrator were common knowledge at the time, familiar to everyone in Spain, including the illiterate. For a modern reader, however, especially one who reads the book in translation or is not conversant with the rich Spanish ballad tradition, the romances are unfamiliar, perhaps exotic, even though they are utterly unproblematic in the intention and structure of the novel. The same is true of allusions to figures and events from the history of Spain—not obscure in and of themselves, but probably not known to most modern readers of *Don Quixote,* regardless of the language in which they read it. For instance, in the course of the novel, Cervantes mentions well-known underworld haunts, famous battle sites and fortresses in North Africa and Europe, popular authors and major military figures of the sixteenth century. These were the kinds of references that I did my best to explain in the notes.

Cervantistas have always loved to disagree and argue, often with venom and vehemence, but I concluded that my primary task was not to become involved in academic disputation or to take sides in any scholarly polemic but to create a translation that could be read with pleasure by as many people as possible. I wanted English-language readers to savor its humor, its melancholy, its originality, its intellectual and esthetic complexity; I wanted them to know why the entire world thinks this is a great masterwork by an incomparable novelist. In the end, my primary consideration was this: *Don Quixote* is not essentially a puzzle for academics, a repository of Renaissance usage, a historical monument, or a text for the classroom. It is a work of literature, and my concern as a literary translator was to create a piece of writing in English that perhaps could be called literature too.

Finally, my formal apology. I would like to cite the last paragraph of my translator's note:

> I began the work in February 2001 and completed it two years later, but it is important for you to know that "final" versions are determined more by a publisher's due date than by any sense on my part that the work is actually finished. Even so, I hope you find it deeply amusing and truly compelling. If not, you can be certain the fault is mine. (xx)

To this I should add a phrase attributed to Samuel Beckett: "Next time I'll have to fail better." That is all any of us can do.

3
translating
poetry

Bring over a poem's ideas and images, and you will lose its manner; imitate prosodic effects, and you sacrifice its matter. Get the letter and you miss the spirit, which is everything in poetry; or get the spirit and you miss the letter, which is everything in poetry. But these are false dilemmas. . . . Verse translation at its best generates a wholly new utterance in the second language—new, yet equivalent, of equal value.

—JOHN FELSTINER,
Translating Neruda

John Felstiner knows more than most about the translation of difficult verse. He not only has translated the poetry of Pablo Neruda and Paul Celan but has written incisively and compellingly, in two brilliant books— *Translating Neruda: The Way to Macchu Picchu,* and *Paul Celan: Poet, Survivor, Jew*—about the process of bringing the work of those poets over into English. Felstiner consistently affirms the intrinsic, independent significance of the successful poetic translation, calling it a literary artifact as noteworthy and estimable as the original piece of writing. The attribution of extreme value to the translation is a concept that has brought me extraordinary aid and comfort at those times when I have been engaged in the overwhelmingly difficult and exceptionally rewarding act of rendering Spanish-language verse in English.

I have always derived immense pleasure from the translation of poetry. My first forays into the work when I was a student at the University of Pennsylvania were well-intended, somewhat pious efforts to transform Spanish poems into English ones for the campus literary magazine. And yet, in spite of that youthful enthusiasm, the main focus of my activity in translation has been prose fiction. What I learned in the early days of my career may help to explain why I did not follow my poetic bliss. When I was starting out as a translator, in the 1970s, the generally accepted rate in New York for the translation of poetry was fifty cents a line. This meant that if you devoted serious, sometimes excruciating amounts of effort, time, and emotional energy to the translation of a sonnet into English, your total fee was seven dollars. No matter how abstemious your needs and wants, no matter how circumspect your financial ambitions, it was clearly impossible to earn even a modest living as a translator of poetry unless you were willing to take an irrevocable vow of poverty (the rates for translating fiction were not much better, but most of the time it was possible to complete a page of prose in about the same time it took to revise and rework a line of poetry—it was, in other words, a more cost-effective enterprise). No wonder the siren song of prose grew louder, sweeter, and increasingly irresistible as I devoted more and more time to translating, until it finally became my full-time occupation some twenty years ago. But over the years I have been fascinated to discover that the translation of artful prose and the translation of poetry are comparable in several significant ways. They both presuppose in the original writing an exquisitely thoughtful use of language to create the many effects that the literary arts are capable of: emotional resonance, conceptual engagement, rhythmic pattern, esthetic tension, and sheer gorgeousness of expression. And they both present analogous challenges to the translator's literary sensibilities and our capacity for entering a text as deeply as possible. The specific experience of translating poetry, with its obligatory attentiveness to the most minute compositional details—linguistic nuance, rhythm, and sound in two languages—enhances immeasurably the approach to the translation of prose, an artistic idiom that has its own nuances, rhythms, and sounds, all of which need to be transferred, their esthetic integrity intact, into a second language.

In spite of these undeniable intergenre connections, I do not believe anyone could, or would even want to, dispute the notion that poetry is the most intense, most highly charged, most artful and complex form of language we have. In many ways it is the essential literary expression of our species, long associated with the distant origins of music, dance, and religious ritual in early human cultures. And yet, although it may be universally human, the inescapable truth is that poetry can seem completely localized, thoroughly contextualized, and absolutely inseparable from the language in which it is written in ways that prose is not. The textures of a language, its musicality, its own specific tradition of forms and meters and imagery, the intrinsic modalities and characteristic linguistic structures that make it possible to express certain concepts, emotions, and responses in a specific manner but not in another—all of these inhere so profoundly in a poem that its translation into another language appears to be an act of rash bravado verging on the foolhardy. Still, we who make that injudicious attempt are the heirs to a long tradition of verse translation. In the modern period, poets like Yves Bonnefoy, Ezra Pound, William Carlos Williams, Charles Baudelaire, Richard Howard, W. S. Merwin, Richard Wilbur, and Charles Simic, to name only a handful, have proclaimed the value of translating poetry by engaging in it themselves, and there is no doubt that by means of translation, poets have had a profound and long-lived influence on writing in other languages: consider, for example, the comprehensive, defining impact of Petrarch on all of Europe in the sixteenth and seventeenth centuries, or of Walt Whitman throughout Latin America in the nineteenth and twentieth, or of Federico García Lorca and Pablo Neruda on poets in the United States after the Second World War. It is almost impossible to imagine what the course of Western poetry would have been without these and many similar cultural and linguistic convergences of poetic form and sensibility. Anne Sexton, for one, was fully aware of this, as cited in an essay by Jonathan Cohen: "We [North American poets] are being influenced now by South American poets, Spanish poets, French poets. We are much more image-driven as a result. . . . Neruda is the great image-maker. The greatest colorist. . . . That's why I say you have to start with Neruda" (25).

It is certainly the case, however, that despite the weight and importance of translated poetry in our literature, the confluence of sound, sense, and form in a poem presents an especially difficult problem in parsing for the translator. How can you separate the inseparable? The simultaneous, indissoluble components of a poetic statement have to be re-created in another language without violating them beyond recognition, but the knotty, perplexing quandary is that in the poet's conception of the work, those elements are not disconnected but are all present at once in the imagining of the poem. Felstiner and Bonnefoy both tell us that in many consequential and meaningful ways the translator continues the process initiated by the poet, searching for the ideal words, the perfect mode of expression needed to create a poem. But in order to achieve this, the translator is obliged to divide constituent parts that were originally indivisible in the poet's conception and, at the same time, move in contrary esthetic directions: the language of the poem, its syntax, lexicon, and structures, by definition have to be altered drastically, even though the work's statement and intention, its emotive content and imagery, must remain the same.

As Felstiner maintains in *Translating Neruda*:

Translating a poem often feels essentially like the primary act of writing, of carrying some preverbal sensation or emotion or thought over into words. Anyone who has slowly shaped an original sentence knows what it feels like to edge toward a word or phrase and then toward a more apt one—one that suddenly touches off a new thought. The same experience holds for poets, generating a line of verse, who find that the right rhyme or image when it comes can trigger an unlooked-for and now indispensable meaning.

So it is in the to-and-fro of verse translation, where finding how and finding why to choose a particular rendering are interdependent. In its own way the translator's activity reenacts the poet's and can form the cutting edge of comprehension. (32)

The how and the why of a "particular rendering" is what I would like to examine with reference to my own experience as a translator of poetry.

The primary concern for me has always been a fairly obvious but deceptively simple question: how would I write the poem if I were composing it in English within the formal constraints set by the poet? These constraints include but are not limited to elements of form such as rhythm, meter, rhyme, stanzaic structure, and line length. I believe that of all these poetic elements, the most important is rhythm. Not all poems employ the specific rhythmic, organizational devices of meter or rhyme or regular stanza divisions, but I think that almost every poem uses rhythmic stresses and their effects to create a powerful, frequently subliminal esthetic pull between the tension of anticipation or expectation and its satisfaction or release. It often seems that this in particular is what people mean when they refer to the music of a verse.

The beat of a line, whether subtle or emphatic, is, to my ear, crucial to both the spirit and the letter of the entire poetic statement. It allows structural coherence even in freewheeling, apparently conversational, almost prosaic verse. As the Irving Mills lyric to Duke Ellington's tune explains, "It don't mean a thing if it ain't got that swing," an insight that holds as true in poetry as it does in jazz.

I have always believed that in the process of rewriting a poem in a second language, it is incumbent upon me as the translator to hear that beat and transfer an equivalent pulse into the English lines. How can one accomplish this when the essential rhythms and metric assumptions of Spanish and English are so different from each other? English, for example, has a much larger number of one-syllable words than Spanish. The effect on the rhythm of the language is incalculable: think of the stunning effect of monosyllables in the poetry of Shakespeare or Hopkins or Yeats. Powerful lines in their work are composed entirely of monosyllables. The final couplet of Shakespeare's Sonnet 147, for example:

For I have sworn thee fair, and thought thee bright,
Who art as black as hell, as dark as night.

And of Sonnet 149:

But, love, hate on, for now I know thy mind;
Those that can see thou lov'st, and I am blind.

In Hopkins's Sonnet 44, the pounding first and eleventh lines

I wake and feel the fell of dark, not day.

Bones built in me, flesh filled, blood brimmed the curse.

And in Yeats, the entire poem "The Lover's Song," with the exception of one word in the last line:

Bird sighs for the air,
Thought for I know not where,
For the womb the seed sighs.
Now sinks the same rest
On mind, on nest,
On straining thighs.

And the first four lines of the second stanza of "Crazy Jane Talks with the Bishop," with the exception of one word in the fourth line:

"Fair and foul are near of kin,
And fair needs foul," I cried.
"My friends are gone, but that's a truth
Nor grave nor bed denied."

Then, too, the metric traditions of the two languages are entirely different: Spanish counts syllables to determine the meter of a line but English counts feet. Despite these obstacles to translation, I begin the attempt to effect the transposition from Spanish to English by reading the poem aloud. Poetry was aural long before it was written and visual, and it seems to me that our ears—mine, at least—are much more sensitive than our eyes to the temporal movement of organized, artful language: its pauses, its convolutions of meaning, its cadences, its musicality. I repeat this procedure, reading the lines aloud, over and over again, until the Spanish patterns have been internalized and I can start to hear in my mind's ear the rhythms of a preliminary English version. Here is where spoken cadences become much more important than formal structures: regardless of whether meter is based on syllable count (Spanish) or on the number of feet per line (English), when the poem is spoken, deep-rooted tempos become audible. When I finally write down a translated version, I read that aloud as well, many more times than once, listening for the authenticity of the English and its synergistic connection to the original, doing my best to have the two mesh until the seams and points of union become invisible. In the best of all possible worlds—one I can rarely reach no matter how much I strive to attain it—the translation stands on independent, English-speaking legs and displays the "equal value" that John Felstiner writes about so compellingly.

At the same time, and just as important to its success, the translation remains faithful to the esthetic and emotive reality of its source and is a consistently true and accurate reflection of the first poem. This means that if all goes well—if the translation succeeds—English-speaking readers have the opportunity to read a convincing poem in their own language, repeating an esthetic experience comparable to that of their Spanish-speaking counterparts.

I would like to discuss briefly the writing of some poets whose work I have translated, presenting both the Spanish original and the English version and analyzing the process that helped determine some of the choices I made in the translation. The discussion is roughly chronological in reverse, beginning with the youngest of the poets.

Jaime Manrique (born in 1949) is a Colombian author who has lived in New York for more than thirty years. He normally writes prose—novels, biographies, and essays—in English, but his poetry is almost always composed in Spanish, and it has been my great pleasure to translate some of his work. This poetry does not conform to the conventions of meter or rhyme in Spanish. Instead, Manrique creates his poetic structure by using colloquial language and a conversational tone to express deeply felt responses to the natural world and nostalgia-filled, yearning memories of people and places (as he says in one of his poems, "I remember that death is not remembering. / I remember; ergo I live"). The sense of loss in his writing is palpable, and the imagery is consistently striking, intense, and unexpected. As always, the significant challenge for me in bringing his poetry over into English has been to maintain the tone, the emotional content, and the intimate, familiar, and sometimes mimetic rhythms of his lines in a translation that feels like equivalent verse in English.

A composition by Manrique in which the translation focused on transferring rhythms and capturing a certain domestic tone is called "Mambo." The original re-creates the dance rhythm of the mambo, using it to highlight the whirling images of the past that flash before the reader's eyes like a series of snapshots. In the translation, I tried to duplicate those dance rhythms and that representational, photographic quality with what is essentially a trimeter (although Spanish meter is not based on feet)—that is, an English version of the three-beat line that dominates the original. (See pages 102–103.) This has always seemed to me an affecting piece of writing. It presents the kind of subjective, emotional connection to a theme or feeling or state of mind that one normally does not encounter in the work of Nicanor Parra, for example, another ordinary-language poet from the opposite end of South America.

Mambo

Contra un cielo topacio
y ventanales estrellados
con delirantes trinitarias
y rojas, sensuales cayenas;
el fragante céfiro vespertino
oloroso de almendros y azahar de la India;
sobre las baldozas de diseños moriscos,
con zapatillas de tacón aguja,
vestidos descotados y amplias polleras;
sus largas, obsidianas cabelleras
a la usanza de la época;
perfumadas, trigueñas, risueñas,
mis tías bailaban el mambo
canturreando, "Doctor, mañana
no me saca ud. la muela,
aunque me muera del dolor."

Aquellas tardes en mi infancia
cuando mis tías eran muchachas y me pertenecían,
y yo bailaba cobijado entre sus polleras,
nuestras vidas eran un mambo feliz
que no se olvida. (30–31)

∎

Nicanor Parra (1914) was the subject of my doctoral dissertation, subsequently published as *The Antipoetry of Nicanor Parra* by New York University Press in 1975. He is the self-termed "antipoet," and consequently, as he has said, anything he chooses to write is "antipoetry." As one would expect, given the

Mambo

Against a topaz sky
and huge windows starry
with delirious heartsease
and sensual red cayenne;
the sweet twilight breeze
fragrant with almond and Indian orange;
on the Moorish tiles,
wearing their spike-heeled sandals,
low cut dresses and wide swirling skirts;
their long obsidian hairdos
in the style of the time;
perfumed, olive-skinned, smiling,
my aunts danced the mambo
and sang: "Doctor, tomorrow,
you can't pull my tooth
even if I die of the pain."

Those evenings of my childhood
when my aunts were young and belonged to me,
and I danced hiding in their skirts,
our lives were a happy mambo—
I remember.

---

implications of a rather loosely defined antipoetic and inten-
tionally provocative esthetic, he regularly eschews traditional
poetic forms. A major literary figure in his native Chile and
throughout Latin America and the rest of the Spanish-speaking
world, he has been prominent since the late 1930s, when his
first volumes of poetry were published. Employing references to

the most mundane objects, burlesque renderings of quotidian experience, and the kind of biting, sardonic wit that sometimes verges on the surreal, Parra, who is fluent in English and has spent significant periods of time in the United States and Great Britain, was heavily influenced by the Beat poets and in turn influenced them (City Lights published English translations of Parra's work as early as 1960, and William Carlos Williams, a

---

El tren instantáneo
(entre Santiago y Puerto Montt)

la locomotora del tren instantáneo
está en el lugar de destino (Puerto Montt)
y el último carro
en el punto de partida (Santiago)

la gran ventaja que presenta este tipo de tren
consiste en que el viajero llega a Puerto Montt
en el instante mismo de abordar el ultimo carro en Santiago

lo único que tiene que hacer a continuación
es trasladarse con sus maletas
x el interior del tren
hasta llegar al primero carro

una vez realizada esta operación
el pasajero puede proceder a bajarse del tren
que ha permanecido inmóvil
durante todo el trayecto

observación: el tren instantáneo sirve solo para viajes de ida. Para volver se necesita un tren inverso. (Parra, 186–187)

kind of tutelary godfather to the Beats, translated poetry by
Parra in the 1950s). Especially in the vindication, or revindica-
tion, of colloquial, ordinary language as a vehicle for poetic
intensity, Parra and poets like Lawrence Ferlinghetti and Allen
Ginsberg had a good deal in common. This shared esthetic
found particular expression in their antiacademic stance, which
had an almost irresistible resonance in the 1950s and 1960s, at

---

Plan for an Instant Train
(between Santiago and Puerto Montt)

the locomotive of the instant train
stands at the destination (Puerto Montt)
while the last car
remains at the point of departure (Santiago)

the advantage of this new train
is that the traveler reaches Puerto Montt
just as he boards the last car in Santiago

all he has to do is simply
walk with his luggage
through the train
until he reaches the first car

once this has been completed
the passenger can proceed to disembark from the train
which has not moved at all
during the entire operation

Note: the instant train can only be used one-way; for return trips a
reversed train is required.

least in the United States. On the other hand, readers of poetry in Latin America, particularly the more conservative critics in Chile, found Parra's experimentation with colloquial style and mordant content absolutely startling, and in some cases shocking. The pleasures of poking at the bourgeoisie never seem to fade, especially when the bourgeoisie appear so willing, even eager, to be offended.

The composition "Plan for an Instant Train" (dated 1984, long after Nicanor Parra's place in the history of Spanish-language poetry had been firmly established) typifies the comically skewed reasoning that runs like a thread through much of his later writing, brilliantly highlighting Parra's deeply satiric take on the abuses of language and logic in contemporary bureaucratic jargon and the social organizations that produce it.

In reading the poem, it is important to remember that a distance of some 630 miles separates the Chilean cities of Santiago and Puerto Montt. In my translation, which attempts to duplicate the humorless, unsmiling prose rhythms of the original, I tried to capture the mindless pomposity of inflated official language. Sadly, both English and Spanish have an abundant supply of the relevant empty terminology.

Unlike Manrique, Parra does not use colloquial language to create nostalgia or feed memory. The poem is completely free of affective language or emotional resonances, unless one wishes to make a case for the unspoken despair any sensible person feels at being exposed to the imbecility of officialdom.

I was confronted by an entirely different set of challenges and considerations when I made my first professional venture into the translation of the classic verse of the Spanish Renaissance.

In 2006 W. W. Norton published *The Golden Age: Poems of the Spanish Renaissance*. The volume includes works by major figures of the fifteenth, sixteenth, and seventeenth centuries, which I selected and translated on the basis of their being some of my favorite poems by some of my favorite poets of the period: Jorge Manrique, Garcilaso de la Vega, Fray Luis de León, San Juan de la Cruz, Luis de Góngora, Lope de Vega, Francisco de Quevedo, and Sor Juana Inés de la Cruz. As I said in my translator's note, this project called upon me to articulate clearly, at least to myself, my deepest vision of what it means to translate a poem:

> The challenge of translating these monumental works was enormous for a good number of reasons, including their overwhelming canonical stature, [and] the inherent problem of bringing over into English a preponderantly rhymed poetry. . . . I had to ponder very carefully the question of how I defined the essence of a poem, how I ought to translate that essence, and how I would fulfill the translator's dual obligation to the original work and to the text in translation. I finally concluded that although separating rhyme from rhythm might well be barbarous, since rhyme is an intrinsic

part of a poem's rhythmic structure, my English versions would be best served if I focused on re-creating meter. (xxvii)

And that is what I did to the best of my ability, concentrating almost exclusively, at least in the early drafts, on the effort at duplication in English of the line lengths of the poems in Spanish. In other words, hendecasyllabic (eleven-syllable) lines in Spanish remained hendecasyllabic in the translation, and the same was true for the other meters, which in this volume were preponderantly heptasyllabic and octosyllabic (seven- and eight-syllable). The hendecasyllables were the least problematic for me to translate in terms of straightforward meter, since the iambic pentameter of English poetry of the Renaissance is, if not a fraternal twin, then at least a first cousin to the Petrarchan eleven-syllable line that had such an overwhelming impact on Spanish poetry in the sixteenth and seventeenth centuries. Iambic pentameter dominates Elizabethan poetry and poetic drama, and innumerable compositions since then. Anyone who reads poetry in English has already begun to internalize, almost unconsciously, the rhythm of that meter, which measures the cadence and pulse of the sonnet as well as a good number of other poetic forms that flourished under the influence of Renaissance Italian verse. The transposition of hendecasyllabic lines into iambic pentameter was a relatively painless process. I found the translation of the shorter verses, the lines with five, seven, or eight syllables, much more problematic; I am not as aware of these meters in English as I am of the more familiar iambic pentameters.

It was also important, in my opinion, to attempt to have the stresses fall on the same syllables in English as in Spanish. Almost all hendecasyllables have an undeviating stress on the tenth syllable, but the placement of other stresses in the line can vary (fourth, eighth, and tenth syllables, for instance, or third, seventh, and tenth), although the approximate center of the line, the sixth syllable, followed by a caesura, or pause, also tends to be accented with great frequency. These two stresses (on the sixth and tenth syllables) are generally constant even when submerged rhythm, like the four-beat line in English (the one found alternating with three-beat lines in nursery rhymes), runs beneath the pentameter and insists on being heard. The rhythms of these poems from the oral tradition are wonderfully consistent:

> Jack and Jill went up the hill
> to fetch a pail of water . . .

> Mary had a little lamb,
> its fleece was white as snow . . .

> A dillar a dollar a ten o'clock scholar
> what makes you come so soon . . .

The native line in Spanish is octosyllabic, which can also have

four beats (this is the meter of the ballads, the romances originally of the oral tradition and later cultivated alongside Petrarchan rhythms, often by the same poets), but I have not
discovered it hiding under the Italianate eleven syllables in the
same way the so-called Anglo-Saxon line, partially obscured by
foreign meters, is there in English. I am not certain why this
should be the case. I wonder whether it is connected to the
Germanic inheritance in English of pounding monosyllabic
words, generally absent in Spanish. This difference naturally
affects the translation of poetry and the rendering of tempo,
since polysyllables in Spanish often have to be expressed by
monosyllabic equivalents in English.

Soneto 145

Este, que ves, engaño colorido,
que del arte ostentando los primores,
con falsos silogismos de colores
es cauteloso engaño del sentido;

      éste, en quien la lisonja ha pretendido
excusar de los años los horrores,
y venciendo del tiempo los rigores,
triunfar de la vejez y del olvido,

      es un vano artificio del cuidado,
es una flor al viento delicada,
es un resguardo inútil para el hado;

      es una necia diligencia errada,
es un afán caduco y, bien mirado,
es cadaver, es polvo, es sombra, es nada. (192–193)

This was certainly true in my translation of the poems in this volume of Golden Age verse. An illustrative example is Sonnet 145 of Sor Juana Inés de la Cruz (1648 or 1651–1695), her famous meditation on a portrait that she considers a flattering evasion of the deepest truths about the transience of youth, beauty, and life itself. I will focus on two lines to exemplify certain devices used throughout the poem.

In the second and third lines of the first strophe, the demands of the meter seem to collide with the essential nature of English and the prevalence of monosyllables in its lexicon. Although all the lines in the Spanish sonnet, with its fixed, tradi-

---

Sonnet 145

This thing you see, a bright-colored deceit,
displaying all the many charms of art,
with false syllogisms of tint and hue
is a cunning deception of the eye;

　　this thing in which sheer flattery has tried
to evade the stark horrors of the years
and, vanquishing the cruelties of time,
to triumph over age and oblivion,

　　is vanity, contrivance, artifice,
a delicate blossom stranded in the wind,
a failed defense against our common fate;

　　a fruitless enterprise, a great mistake,
a decrepit frenzy, and rightly viewed,
a corpse, some dust, a shadow, mere nothingness.

tional rhyme scheme (ABBA ABBA CDC DCD), are feminine, or grave, with the stress falling on the penultimate or next-to-last syllable, in the English translation all but three of the lines are masculine, or acute, with the stress on the final syllable. For the most part, that accentuation is based on the presence of monosyllabic line endings. One of the effects, I think, of the three polysyllabic endings in lines 8, 9, and 14, is to give special emphasis to the central thematic thread or statement of the poem: "oblivion," "artifice," and "nothingness."

In line 2 I did not intend the words *all* and *many,* not present in Spanish, as a kind of filler or padding (as one reviewer claimed) to cushion the impact of Sor Juana's incisive writing or to ameliorate her trenchant vision of the contrast between the relative permanence of the portrait and the inevitable passing of her corporeal life. They are there to create the rhythm in English that I felt was essential to the translation, but they do not change the significance of the line in any consequential way. The same is true in line 3, where the synonyms *tint* and *hue* create the tempo achieved by a single word in Spanish (*colores*) but do not change essential meaning. In every case, the addition or deletion of words in the translation was motivated by what was, for me, the prodigious importance of maintaining rhythmic structure.

In Sonnet CLXV of Luis de Góngora (1561–1627), as in the

sonnet by Sor Juana, the rhyme scheme is traditional (ABBA ABBA CDC EDE) and the line endings are paroxytonic, or feminine, while all but two of the line endings in English are masculine, or oxytonic. (See pages 114–115.) The alterations I needed to make to achieve comparable rhythms in the translation are somewhat less apparent or radical than in the sonnet by Sor Juana. Here they tend to be confined to the addition or omission of small, one-syllable words, except for the penultimate line of the final tercet, where the demands of English syntax required more significant changes.

In the first and fourth lines of the first quatrain, for example, the English omits the monosyllabic *y*, equivalent to English *and*. In the second line of the first tercet, again for the sake of rhythm, the word *obscura*, equivalent to English *dark*, is lengthened to *darkest* to gain a needed syllable. In these cases, I believe there was little or no substantive modification to the effect of the line or its meaning. In the last tercet, however, I could think of no way to express the image in comprehensible English and within the imagistic and metaphorical parameters of the line except to add the words "with its own snowy," which do not appear in equivalent form in Spanish. Again, in spite of this considerable amplification in the translation, to my mind the intent of the poem was not transformed, and the passionate tempo of its statement was not lost.

■

In the poems I included in the Norton anthology, the translation of the shorter lines—the ones with five, seven, or eight
syllables, traditional native meters of Spain that remained current throughout the Renaissance—was, as I have indicated,
considerably more difficult for me, since comparable lines do
not have the same presence and weight in English as the iambic
pentameter. Still, these meters do tend to generate rhythms that
could be transferred to the English versions.

"Décima," a short poem by Fray Luis de León (1527–1591),
written after his release from the prisons of the Inquisition, is
based on the ten-line stanzaic form called the *décima,* which
was used by countless Renaissance poets in Spain. Written in

Soneto CLXV

    Ilustre y hermosísima María,
mientras se dejan ver a cualquier hora
en tus mejillas la rosada Aurora,
Febo en tus ojos y en tu frente el día,

    y mientras con gentil descortesía
mueve el viento la hebra voladora
que la Arabia en sus venas atesora
y el rico Tajo en sus arenas cría;

    antes que, de la edad Febo eclipsado
y el claro día vuelto en noche obscura,
huya la Aurora del mortal nublado;

    antes que lo que hoy es rubio tesoro
venza a la blanca nieve su blancura:
goza, goza el color, la luz, el oro. (140–141)

octosyllables, it has a variable rhyme scheme and a customary shift in the pattern of rhyme after the fifth line. It is used here by Fray Luis in a version of the theme of *Beatus Ille,* a term derived from an ode by the Roman poet Horace. (See pages 116–117.) This poetic motif praises the tranquility and peace endemic to the countryside in contrast to the political scheming and seductive spiritual dangers of an urban environment, the court in particular, and it remained popular for centuries in European lyric and drama. "Happy the man [who lives in the country]" is a rough translation of the Latin phrase.

The tempo of these lines tends toward three beats, and in the English I did my best to duplicate that trimeter. In line

---

Sonnet CLXV

Luminous, most beautiful María,
as long as we can see at any hour
rosy-hued Aurora upon your cheek,
Phoebus in your eyes, day upon your brow,

and as long as the wind, so gently rude,
breathes upon and tousles those wafting threads
that Arabia hoards and treasures in its veins,
and wealthy Tagus gives us in its sands,

before bright Phoebus is eclipsed by time,
and clear day changes into darkest night,
making Aurora flee the mortal cloud;

before what is today blond treasure conquers
with its own snowy whiteness the white snow:
revel, revel in color, light, and gold.

Décima
Al Salir de la Cárcel

Aquí la envidia y mentira
me tuvieron encerrado.
Dichoso el humilde estado
del sabio que se retira
de aqueste mundo malvado,
y con pobre mesa y casa,
en el campo deleitoso
con solo Dios se compasa,
y a solas su vida pasa,
ni envidiado ni envidioso.

---

4 the word *enough* was added to the translation to create the necessary rhythm and to stress the volitional quality of the choice to withdraw from the city; in line 5, the words *spite* and *venom'd* are both implied by the single word *malvado*, divided here into two words for the sake of the eight-syllable, three-beat line.

In this poem, and in the other works translated for the anthology, I was fascinated to discover how careful, perhaps obsessive attention to rhythm and meter often creates the impression of rhyme, frequently through the creation of slant rhymes, also known as half rhymes or near rhymes. Under the best of circumstances, in what John Felstiner calls the "to and fro of verse translation," a balance seems to be created between what is

Stanza

Upon Leaving Prison

Here is where envy and lies
had me imprisoned for years.
Oh happy the humble state
of the man wise enough to flee
the spite of this venom'd world,
and with humble hearth and home
in the pleasant countryside,
and God as his sole companion,
he shuns the presence of men,
not envious, and envied by none. (104–105)

---

sacrificed when the original language is left behind and what is gained in the new language of the translation.

I can think of no better way to conclude this essay than to transcribe Alastair Reid's poetic comment on the inherent dilemma of writing poetry and the intrinsic predicament of translating it. Reid's poem encapsulates for me the endless quandary of writing and of writing as a translator.

■

Lo Que Se Pierde / What Gets Lost

I keep translating traduzco continuamente
entre palabras words que no son las mías
into other words which are mine de palabras a mis palabras.
Y, finalmente, de quién es el texto? Who has written it?
Del escritor o del traductor writer, translator
o de los idiomas or language itself?
Somos fantasmas, nosotros traductores, que viven
entre aquel mundo y el nuestro
between that world and our own.
Pero poco a poco me ocurre
que el problema the problem no es cuestión
de lo que se pierde en traducción
is not a question
of what gets lost in translation
sino but rather lo que se pierde
what gets lost
entre la ocurrencia—sea de amor o de desesperación
between love or desperation—
y el hecho de que llega
a existir en palabras
and its coming into words.

Para nosotros todos, amantes, habladores
as lovers or users of words
el problema es éste this is the difficulty.
Lo que se pierde what gets lost
no es lo que se pierde en traducción sino
is not what gets lost in translation, but rather
what gets lost in language itself lo que se pierde
en el hecho, en la lengua,
en la palabra misma.

Reid understands in the deepest way the ontological risk that defines an intense love relationship with language. That is why I framed the signed copy of this wonderful poem, which he gave to me several years ago, and keep it hanging on the wall of my study: to cheer and encourage me when I am obliged to confront the formidable, irresistible act of translation.

A Personal List of Important Translations

The books listed here are not necessarily the best or most recent translations of works originally written in another language, but most were ones I acquired when I was a student. The majority of them are inexpensive paperbacks or hardbacks purchased in secondhand bookstores. I still own them, many yellowed and tattered, and each brings with it a memory of the excitement of my first reading—the beginning of my exploration of the world beyond the borders of English.

This is not intended as a comprehensive record of all the translations that have mattered to me, but I think it is fair to say that these made a deep and long-lasting impression and certainly influenced the way I write and translate. Then too, I still own them and can find the volumes on my book shelves—something I could never do if I attempted to reconstruct the titles and their translators from memory.

Finally, it is obvious that the books by Sebald and Saramago came out long after I was a student, but I read them both for the first time in the same year, and the impact was overwhelming.

- The Bible in the King James version
- Sophocles, *Oedipus the King,* trans. David Grene
- Sophocles, *Oedipus at Colonnus,* trans. Robert Fitzgerald
- Sophocles, *Antigone,* trans. Elizabeth Wyckoff
- Aeschylus, the *Oresteia,* trans. Richard Lattimore
- Ovid, *The Art of Love,* trans. Rolfe Humphries
- Homer, *The Odyssey,* trans. E. V. Rieu. This is a prose translation that I remember using as a pony when I read Joyce's *Ulysses*
- Plato, *The Symposium,* trans. W. Hamilton
- Dante, *The Divine Commedy,* trans. John Ciardi
- Cervantes, *Don Quixote,* trans. Samuel Putnam. I read this before I knew enough of the language to read the book in Spanish.
- Nietzsche, *Thus Spake Zarathustra,* trans. Thomas Common
- Marx and Engels, *The Communist Manifesto,* trans. anonymous! (though according to the text on the cover, this is the "authorized English translation")
- Stendhal, *Scarlet and Black,* trans. Margaret R. B. Shaw

- Stendhal, *The Charterhouse of Parma,* trans. C. K. Scott Moncrieff
- Flaubert, *Madame Bovary,* trans. Eleanor Marx-Aveling
- Dostoevsky, *Crime and Punishment,* trans. David Magarshack
- Dostoevsky, *The Brothers Karamazov,* trans. Constance Garnett
- Tolstoy, *War and Peace,* trans. Rosemary Edmonds
- Tolstoy, *Anna Karenina,* trans. Constance Garnett
- Gogol, *Dead Souls,* trans. Bernard Guilbert Guerney
- Chekhov, selected plays, trans. Elisaveta Fen
- Machado de Assis, *Epitaph of a Small Winner,* trans. William L. Grossman
- Mann, *Buddenbrooks,* trans. H. T. Lowe Porter
- Mann, *The Magic Mountain,* trans. H. T. Lowe Porter
- Mann, *Death in Venice,* trans. H. T. Lowe Porter
- Rilke, *Sonnets to Orpheus,* trans. C. F. MacIntyre
- Rilke, *Duino Elegies,* trans. C. F. MacIntyre
- Rilke, *Selected Poems,* trans. C. F. MacIntyre
- Grass, *The Tin Drum,* trans. anonymous—the name of the translator is nowhere to be found!
- Kundera, *The Unbearable Lightness of Being,* trans. Michael Henry Heim
- Kazantzakis, *The Last Temptation of Christ,* trans. P. A. Bien

- Saramago, *The Year of the Death of Ricardo Reis,* trans. Giovanni Pontiero
- Saramago, *Manual of Painting and Calligraphy,* trans. Giovanni Pontiero
- Saramago, *The Cave,* trans. Margaret Jull Costa
- Saramago, *Blindness,* trans. Giovanni Pontiero
- Saramago, *Seeing,* trans. Margaret Jull Costa
- Saramago, *The History of the Siege of Lisbon,* trans. Giovanni Pontiero
- Saramago, *Death with Interruption,* trans. Margaret Jull Costa
- Sebald, *The Rings of Saturn,* trans. Michael Hulse
- Sebald, *The Emigrants,* trans. Michael Hulse
- Sebald, *Vertigo,* trans. Michael Hulse
- Sebald, *Austerlitz,* trans. Anthea Bell
- Sebald, *Campo Santo,* trans. Anthea Bell
- Sartre, *Anti-Semite and Jew,* trans. George J. Becker

I knew enough French and Italian to read most nineteenth- and twentieth-century poetry in the original language.

works cited

Alcalay, Ammiel. Introduction to Miljenko Jergović, *Sarajevo Marlboro,* trans. Stela Tomašević. New York: Archipelago, 2004.

Benjamin, Walter. "The Task of the Translator," trans. Harry Zohn. In Schulte and Biguenet, *Theories of Translation,* 71–82.

Cervantes, Miguel de. *Don Quijote de la Mancha,* ed. Martín de Riquer. Barcelona: Editorial Juventud, 1971.

Cohen, Jonathan. "Neruda in English: Establishing His Residence in U.S. Poetry." *Multicultural Review* 13, no. 4 (2004): 25–28.

Dryden, John. "On Translation." In Schulte and Biguenet, *Theories of Translation,* 17–31.

Dubus, Andre, III. Introduction to *Words Without Borders: The World Through the Eyes of Writers,* ed. Samantha Schnee, Alane Salierno Mason, and Dedi Felman, xi–xvi. New York: Anchor, 2007.

Felstiner, John. *Translating Neruda: The Way to Macchu Picchu.* Stanford: Stanford University Press, 1980.

García Márquez, Gabriel. *Living to Tell the Tale,* trans. Edith Grossman. New York: Knopf, 2003.

Grossman, Edith. Translator's note to Miguel de Cervantes, *Don Quixote,* xvii–xx. New York: Ecco/HarperCollins, 2003.

———, trans. *The Golden Age: Poems of the Spanish Renaissance.* New York: Norton, 2006.

Manrique, Jaime. "Mambo." In *My Night with/Mi noche con Federico García Lorca,* trans. Edith Grossman and Eugene Richie. Hudson, N.Y.: Groundwater, 1995.

Monterroso, Augusto. "How I Got Rid of Five Hundred Books." In *Complete Works and Other Stories,* trans. Edith Grossman, 117–121. Austin: University of Texas Press, 1995.

Nabokov, Vladimir. "Problems of Translation: *Onegin* in English." In Schulte and Biguenet, *Theories of Translation,* 127–143.

Ortega y Gasset, José. "The Misery and the Splendor of Translation," trans. Elizabeth Gamble Miller. In Schulte and Biguenet, *Theories of Translation,* 93–112.

Parra, Nicanor. "Plan for an Instant Train," trans. Edith Grossman. In *Antipoems: New and Selected,* ed. David Unger. New York: New Directions, 1985.

Paz, Octavio. "Translation: Literature and Letters," trans. Irene del Corral. In Schulte and Biguenet, *Theories of Translation,* 152–162.

Sánchez, Luis Rafael. *Indiscreciones de un perro gringo.* Guaynabo, Puerto Rico: Ediciones Santillana, 2007.

Schulte, Rainier, and John Biguenet, eds. *Theories of Translation: An Anthology of Essays from Dryden to Derrida.* Chicago: University of Chicago Press, 1992.

Wechsler, Robert. *Performing Without a Stage: The Art of Literary Translation,* North Haven, Conn.: Catbird, 1998.

acknowledgments

Two dear friends, Jonathan Cohen and Anne Humpherys, helped me immeasurably with their astute, insightful readings of portions of this book. They have my love and deepest gratitude for their friendship.

I am also grateful for permission to reprint the poems that appear here in their entirety:

Jaime Manrique, "Mambo," *My Night with Federico García Lorca / Mi noche con Federico García Lorca* (Madison: University of Wisconsin Press). © 2003 by the Board of Regents of the University of Wisconsin System. Reprinted by permission of The University of Wisconsin Press.

Nicanor Parra, "El tren instantáneo," *Antipoems: New and Selected* (New York: New Directions, 1985). © 1985 by Edith

Grossman. Used by permission of New Directions Publishing Corp.

Sor Juana Inés de la Cruz, Soneto 145; Luis de Góngora, Soneto CLXV; and Fray Luis de León, "Décima," *Renaissance and Baroque Poetry of Spain,* ed. Elias L. Rivers (New York: Scribner, 1966). Translated in *The Golden Age: Poems of the Spanish Renaissance* (New York: Norton, 2006). © 2006 by Edith Grossman. Used by permission of W. W. Norton and Company, Inc.

Alastair Reid, "Lo Que Se Pierde / What Gets Lost." © Alastair Reid. Used by permission of the author.

index

Faulkner, William, 17–21; *Absalom, Absalom,* 18; *Light in August,* 18; *The Sound and the Fury,* 18

Felstiner, John, 76, 89, 91, 95–96, 99, 116; *Paul Celan,* 91; *Translating Neruda,* 91

Ferlinghetti, Lawrence, 104

Fernández, Macedonio, "The Surgery of Psychic Removal," 4–5

fiction, translation of, 9, 41, 92–93. *See also* literature

fidelity, in translation, 31, 67, 69–71, 99

Fielding, Henry, 20

Flaubert, Gustave, 24, 77–78

footnotes, 86–87

France, 59

Franco, Francisco, 53

freedom of communication, 52–54, 60

Frost, Robert, 64

Fuentes, Carlos, 18, 21

Gaelic, 57

García Lorca, Federico, 94

García Márquez, Gabriel, 17–19, 21; *The Autumn of the Patriarch,* 46–47; *Living to Tell the Tale,* 18, 45, 81; *La mala hora,* 45; *One Hundred Years of Solitude,* 18, 72

Gavronsky, Serge, 49–50

Ginsberg, Allen, 104

Goethe, Johann Wolfgang von, 22

Gogol, Nikolay, 25

The Golden Age, 107

Góngora, Luis de, 107; "Sonnet CLXV," 112–114

Green, Otis, 80

Greene, Graham, 18, 24

Grossman, Edith, *The Antipoetry of Nicanor Parra,* 101

hearing. *See* sound

Hemingway, Ernest, 24

hendecasyllabic lines, 107–109

Hopkins, Gerard Manley, 97–98

Horace, 115

Howard, Richard, 94

humanity: poetry and, 93; translation's importance for, 32–33, 38–39, 66–67. *See also* civilization, translation's contribution to

Huxley, Aldous, 18

iambic pentameter, 108–109

imagination, 76–77

independence: of created work, 77; of translation, 91, 99

individualism, 49–51

interpretation, translation and, 73–74

Irish, William, 18

Irish language influence on American English, 57

Edith Grossman is an award-winning translator of Latin American and Spanish literature, ranging from an acclaimed translation of *Don Quixote* and poetry of the Spanish Golden Age to contemporary works by Gabriel García Márquez, Antonio Muñoz Molina, and Carlos Fuentes. The recipient of Woodrow Wilson, Fulbright, and Guggenheim fellowships, Grossman was awarded the PEN/Ralph Manheim Medal for Translation in 2006, in 2007 she received an award in literature from the American Academy of Arts and Letters, and in 2009 she was elected to the American Academy of Arts and Sciences.

She lives in Manhattan and has two sons, both of whom are musicians.

WITHDRAWN